HIGHWAY TO HEAVEN SERIES
EDWARD A. FITZPATRICK, *Editor*
Institute of Catechetical Research, Marquette University

THE LIFE OF MY SAVIOR

HIGHWAY TO HEAVEN SERIES

BOOK OF THE HOLY CHILD (Grade One)

LIFE OF MY SAVIOR (Grade Two)

LIFE OF THE SOUL (Grade Three)

BEFORE CHRIST CAME (Grade Four)

THE VINE AND THE BRANCHES (Grade Five)

THE MISSAL (Grade Six)

HIGHWAY TO GOD (Grades Seven and Eight)

Accompanying this Series is the RELIGION IN LIFE CURRICULUM for grades one to six and PRACTICAL PROBLEMS IN RELIGION for grades seven and eight.

HIGHWAY TO HEAVEN SERIES II

THE LIFE
OF MY
SAVIOR

BY
A SCHOOL SISTER OF NOTRE DAME

Edited by
EDWARD A. FITZPATRICK

St. Augustine Academy Press
Homer Glen, Illinois

Nihil obstat:
H. B. RIES,
Censor librorum

Imprimatur:
✠ SAMUEL A. STRITCH,
Archiepiscopus Milwaukiensis

September 11, 1933

Grateful acknowledgment is hereby made for permission to print or to adapt copyrighted material to the following: Reverend C. A. Burns, S.J., John Carroll University, Cleveland, for "To a Little Boy"; The Devin-Adair Company, New York City, for "A Mother's Quest," "I Know Who is Hiding," and "Jesus on the Cross"; The Macmillan Company, New York City, for "In Church," by Marion D. Thayer; Rev. Felix Kirsch, O.M.Cap., Washington, for poems selected from "Practical Aids for Catholic Teachers." Special thanks are given to Reverend Alton Scheid, Chaplain of Good Counsel Academy, Mankato, Minnesota; to Reverend William Griffin, D.D., Mapleton, Minnesota, for having read most carefully and critically the manuscript; to Dr. Edward A. Fitzpatrick, Dean of the Graduate School, Marquette University, for his untiring efforts and coöperation, making this work possible, to my religious Superiors for their sympathetic encouragement and deep interest.

This book was originally published in 1933 by The Bruce Publishing Company.
This edition reprinted in 2017 by St. Augustine Academy Press
based on the 1935 second printing.

Softcover ISBN: 978-1-64051-022-7
Hardcover ISBN: 978-1-64051-023-4

THIS BOOK BELONGS TO A LITTLE
CHILD WHOM JESUS LOVES AND
WHO LOVES JESUS ABOVE ALL ELSE

_____
Name of Child

THE GREATEST STORIES EVER TOLD

To the Children:[1]

This book tells the greatest stories that were ever told. They are true stories. They tell about God and how He sent His Son, Jesus Christ, to save men. No words but the greatest can describe these stories.

One is called the grandest story ever told because it tells of the grand events of the Creation of the world and of man.

Another story is called the sweetest story because it tells the story of the gentle Mary, the mother, and of the simple Child Jesus, who is God.

Still another story tells how this simple Child, grown up now to be a man, makes the winds and the sea obey Him. It tells how He

---

[1] To be read by the teacher and talked about by the children.

cures the sick, makes the lame walk, the blind see, and even raises men from the dead. This is truly the most wonderful story ever told.

Another story is sadder than any other story ever told about any man. It tells us of how this Lover of Men, who came down from heaven to help and save men, was beaten and nailed to a cross by the very men He came to save. This is, without doubt, the saddest story ever told.

There is a story of how Christ crucified, dead, and buried in a sepulcher, raised Himself from the dead and lived for forty days on earth. This is called the Resurrection. It sealed the work of saving men for which Christ came to earth. This is surely the most glorious story ever told.

One thing remained to be done. Christ, before He ascended into heaven to God, His Father, provides for a way to help men to find the Highway to Heaven. He would send the Holy Ghost. He did. With the coming of the Holy Ghost the Holy Roman Catholic Church had its beginning. This is the holiest story ever told, as it provided a means to make holy and saintly all men throughout all ages. This means is the Holy Roman Catholic Church.

These are truly the greatest stories ever told. Among them is the grandest, the sweetest, the most wonderful, the saddest, the most glorious, and the holiest story that has ever been told to, or heard by men. They are true stories. They happened on earth. They are the life of our Savior, Jesus Christ. They will help you keep on God's Highway and find your home in heaven at the end of it.

EDWARD A. FITZPATRICK

GOD MADE THE WORLD

PART I. THE GRANDEST STORY EVER TOLD

GOD THE CREATOR

Did you ever think about who made the sky, the sun, the birds, the sea? These stories will tell you how great God, the Creator of heaven and earth, is. Read them to your parents.

* * *

1. GOD MADE HEAVEN

It was a long, long time ago. It was so long ago, only God knows. He was all alone, only God, GOD, GOD!

Suddenly God did a grand thing. He made heaven.

Heaven, the beautiful home of God, will be my home, too. God wants me in heaven with Him forever and ever!

GOD MADE THE ANGELS

God did a wonderful thing again.

He wanted angels in His heaven.

Suddenly angels were made! They praised God their Creator and sang:

      Holy, Holy, Holy!
      Great God of Heaven!

The beautiful angels adored God who had made them.

SOMETHING TO DO

Find a picture of angels. Tell little sister or brother about the angels.

2. GOD MADE THE WORLD

After God made heaven and the angels, He made the big, beautiful world.

But it was all dark.

"Let there be LIGHT!" God said. And light was made!

"Let there be sun, moon, stars, seas, birds, trees, hills!" God said again. And they were all made!

God saw all the things He had made, and they were very good.

SOMETHING TO DO

Find pictures of things that God made. Make a picture book of them. Write under each picture: God made the................(birds).

On your way home from school, talk with your little friends about the things you see that God has made.

3. GOD MADE MAN

Once more the great Creator spoke. He said: "Let Us make MAN!" God made a beautiful body from the earth. He breathed a SOUL into this body, and Adam was made!

Adam was the first man on earth. He adored God who had made him. God did not want

Adam to be alone. He said: "Let Us make Adam a help like to himself."

When Adam was asleep, God took one of his ribs. He made another beautiful body from this rib. He breathed a SOUL into this body, and Eve was made!

Eve was the first woman on earth. She adored God who had made her. God loved Adam and Eve. He gave them the Garden of Paradise to be their own beautiful home. Here they were very, very happy.

SOMETHING TO DO

Make the Garden of Paradise on the sand table. Put into it some of the things God made.

Make the Garden of Paradise in your playroom. Ask little brother to help you. Make it very beautiful.

Play that you are Adam and your little friend is Eve. Talk about God and about your home in the Garden. Ask your little friends to play that they are the birds, the flowers, or the lambs in the Garden of Paradise.

4. GOD MADE ME

God gave the dearest gifts to Adam and Eve, many happy little boys and girls. God made all the little children on the whole earth. About seven years ago, God made another beautiful little baby. He gave it to a very sweet mother and a very kind father. They would take good care of it for God.

Who was that wonderful little baby? Why, it was I, I! God made me! He made my eyes, my hands, my whole body. He breathed a SOUL into my little body, and I was made!

My soul will live forever and ever. God loves my soul more than anything else on this earth.

God made me for His home, heaven. One day He will say to me: "Come, My child, into heaven. I want you with Me forever and ever. I made you just for Myself, for heaven!"

SOME THINGS TO TALK ABOUT WITH YOUR FATHER

How good God is to ME!
God made me.
God loves me very much.
God gave me good parents.
God wants me to know Him. How can I?
God wants me to love Him. How can I?
God wants me to serve Him. How can I?

MY GUARDIAN ANGEL WATCHES OVER ME

5. MY GUARDIAN ANGEL

God made an angel just for me. This angel is always with me. He watches over me all the day and all the night. The poem is about my Guardian Angel.

* * *

Guardian Angel, are you here
Close beside me, Angel dear?
Will you stay with me all day,
Be with me in work and play?
Don't you ever long to be
With angel-folk, instead of me?
Dear Angel, if you ever roam
To your starry heaven-home,
Take me with you, Angel sweet,
Kneel with me at Jesus' feet.

—*School Sister of Notre Dame*

SOMETHING TO DO

Read the poem to your little sister. Tell her about her own Guardian Angel.

Every night and every morning speak a few words to your Guardian Angel.

6. GOD'S LOVING PROMISE

God made a wonderful promise to Adam and Eve. This story tells you about it.

* * *

A most beautiful tree grew in the Garden of Paradise. There were many other trees, too.

God said to Adam: "Of every tree of Paradise you may eat. Of this tree you may not eat!"

Adam and Eve loved God their Father and Creator. They promised to obey Him.

One day the devil was in this tree.

Eve was walking in the Garden, thinking of God. She passed near the tree.

The devil said to Eve: "Why has God told you not to eat of every tree in Paradise?"

Eve said to him: "We do eat of every tree, only not of this one. If we eat the fruit of this tree, we must die."

"No, you shall not die. You shall be like God, if you eat of it," the devil told her.

Then Eve took the fruit, and she gave some to Adam.

Oh, Adam and Eve did not obey God. They did eat of the fruit of this tree. They sinned against God, their kind, loving Father.

JESUS IS GOD'S LOVING PROMISE

Suddenly they became very much afraid and tried to hide from God. God knew what they had done. His own children had sinned against Him. Now they must die.

God sent Adam and Eve out of the beautiful Garden of Paradise. He closed the gates of heaven to them and to all their children. God still loved Adam and Eve and had pity on them. He gave them a Loving Promise.

Jesus, His own Son, would become man.

Jesus would be the Savior of men.

Mary would be the Mother of Jesus.

Jesus is the Loving Promise of God to men.

SOMETHING TO TELL

Tell the story of the Loving Promise to your parents.

Tell how you can thank God for the Loving Promise.

Who made you? Why?

What else did He make?

Is anything hard for God to do?

Who is God?

Will your soul ever die?

Did Adam and Eve fall into sin?

PART II. THE SWEETEST STORY EVER TOLD

1. THE VIRGIN MARY

The Virgin Mary is born.

* * *

More than four thousand years had passed. Heaven was closed all this time. People prayed and prayed, asking God to send the Savior and His Mother.

One day God made a wonderful little girl. He breathed a most beautiful, pure, holy soul into her body. This little girl would be the Mother of the Savior. That is why God made her soul and her body so beautiful.

Joachim and Ann were very holy old people. God gave this little girl to them. She was their own sweet baby. They called her Mary.

The Blessed Virgin Mary had come to earth!

Soon Jesus, the Loving Promise of God, would come, too. He would open the gates of heaven again.

Oh, sweet Virgin Mary, how glad I am that you have come to earth!

2. MARY AND THE ANGEL

The Virgin Mary soon became a beautiful, young woman. A wonderful thing happened to her. The story tells you what it was.

* * *

It was all quiet, very quiet. The beautiful Mary was praying to God.

THE ANGEL APPEARS TO MARY

Suddenly a bright light filled the room. An angel of God stood before her. The angel's name was Gabriel.

The angel bowed low before Mary.

"Hail, full of grace," he said to her. "The Lord is with thee. Blessed art thou among women!"

Mary was afraid.

"Fear not, Mary!" said Gabriel. "Thou shalt have a Son. Thou shalt call His Name JESUS. He shall be called the SON OF THE MOST HIGH."

Mary was not afraid any more. She believed the words of the angel. Now she knew that God wanted her to be the Mother of the Savior.

Then Mary said these holy words: "I am the Handmaid of the Lord!" Mary bowed low in prayer to God. The Angel Gabriel returned to God in heaven with the great, grand message.

WOULD YOU LIKE TO DO THIS?

Act out with your friend the story of the angel and the Virgin Mary.

3. MARY AND ELIZABETH

This story tells you how good Mary was to an old lady.

* * *

Elizabeth was a holy old lady in the land of Israel.

God was sending her a little son. His name was to be John.

Elizabeth was a cousin of the beautiful Mary. The angel had told Mary that Elizabeth would soon have a little son, too.

Mary loved her holy old cousin. She would go into the hill country to visit her and to help her get ready for the little John.

Mary made a journey of many days through the hill country.

At last she came to the home of Elizabeth.

God had told Elizabeth that Mary would be the Mother of the Savior.

When Elizabeth saw Mary, she cried out to her: "Blessed art thou among women!"

Then Mary sang that most beautiful song to God called the *Magnificat*. It was the sweetest song that God had ever heard from earth.

For many, many days, Mary helped her cousin.

Soon her own Baby Boy would be born! She returned to her home in Nazareth where St. Joseph was waiting for her.

What a wonderful visit this was for Elizabeth and her family!

SOMETHING TO DRAW

Draw the hill country which Mary visited.

Draw the home of Elizabeth in the hill country. Tell this story to your mother and show her your picture.

4. NO ROOM IN THE INN

Soon Mary had to make another journey. Would you like to go on this journey with Mary? Then read the story.

* * *

The Blessed Virgin Mary and St. Joseph lived in a little house in Nazareth. Here they waited for the Baby Jesus.

One day Joseph hurried home from work.

"Mary," he said, "we must go to Bethlehem. The king commands it."

And Mary answered St. Joseph: "Let us obey. It is the Will of God."

Mary knew that the Baby Jesus would come very soon. She took some clothes along for her little Jesus.

Soon Joseph and Mary were on their way to Bethlehem.

The journey was hard and long. On, on, over the hills, Mary and Joseph hurried to Bethlehem.

Late one night they came to Bethlehem. They were very, very tired.

Joseph went to the inn.

"Please, sir, will you give us a room for the night?" Joseph asked.

"There is no room in the inn," the people told him.

Poor Joseph and Mary! They went from house to house. They always heard the same words: "No room!"

Baby Jesus wanted to be born that night. But, oh, there was no room in any house for His sweet Mother Mary.

At last they went to a stable on the hillside.

Here Jesus, the Savior of Men, would be born.

5. CHRIST, THE SAVIOR, IS BORN

This is the sweetest story ever told.

* * *

The night was cold and still. The stars were twinkling in the sky as if they knew something beautiful was going to happen. All Bethlehem was sleeping.

It was quiet and dark in the stable. The Blessed Virgin Mary was praying to God.

Suddenly a beautiful light filled the stable.

JESUS, the Son of God, WAS BORN! He was in the arms of His Mother Mary.

Mary adored Jesus, her own sweet God!

Joseph adored Jesus. He bowed low before his God!

Angels came down from heaven and adored their God. They sang so sweetly to Baby Jesus!

Mary wrapped the Infant in swaddling clothes and laid Him in a manger.

This was the very first Christmas.

Some poor shepherds were watching their sheep on the hillside.

THE SHEPHERDS ADORED JESUS

All was dark, only the stars were still twinkling in the sky.

Suddenly a bright light filled the sky. An angel of the Lord appeared before the shepherds.

They were very, very much afraid.

The angel said to them: "Fear not! This day is born to you a Savior, who is Christ the Lord. You shall find the Infant wrapped in swaddling clothes and lying in a manger."

Many angels appeared in the sky. They sang:

"Glory to God in the highest!

Peace on earth to men of good will."

After the song the angels returned to heaven. All was dark and quiet again.

"Let us go over to Bethlehem," the shepherds said to each other.

They hurried over to Bethlehem.

They found the Infant Jesus wrapped in swaddling clothes and lying in the manger. They adored their God.

SOMETHING TO DO

Act out the story of the angels and the shepherds with your little friends.

Act out the story of the shepherds going to the stable and kneeling before the Infant Jesus.

6. BABY JESUS IN THE TEMPLE

This story tells you about Baby Jesus in the Temple.

* * *

Jesus was forty days old.

Mother Mary and St. Joseph brought the Infant Jesus to the Temple to offer Him to God. Baby Jesus offered His own life to God.

Simeon, an old man, was praying in the Temple.

Once upon a time God had made a promise to old Simeon. He would see the Savior of men before he died!

He saw Mother Mary with Jesus in her arms.

At this moment God told him in prayer that this Baby was the Savior of the world.

The old man at once came and adored Jesus.

He took the Infant into his arms. Jesus blessed him and made him happy.

Now the old man was happy to die because he had seen Jesus, the Savior of men!

SOMETHING TO DO

Talk about the pictures you can see in this story.

7. A PLAY ABOUT THREE KINGS

TIME: The First Christmas.

CHARACTERS: The Three Kings, and Jesus, Mary, Joseph, and an Angel.

Scene I. In the Desert

(*The Three Kings meet in the desert. They bow low to each other.*)

FIRST KING: Hail, hail to you, great Kings!

SECOND KING: Hail to you!

THIRD KING (*looking to the sky*): See, the star of the greatest King. Let us follow the star and adore Him.

FIRST KING: I have seen His star in the East. I will follow it.

THIRD KING: I, too, have seen His star. I will follow it until I find the King.

ALL (*to God*): King of Heaven and Earth, we follow Thy star!

(*They again get up on their camels and go to Jerusalem.*)

Scene II. In Jerusalem

(*The Three Kings have come to Herod, the

wicked King who rules over the Jews. The Kings bow low before Herod.)

HEROD: I am pleased, great Kings, to see you. What can I do for you?

FIRST KING: We have come to adore the new-born King of the Jews. Will you take us to Him?

HEROD (*very much afraid*): Why, there is no new King of the Jews. I am the King!

SECOND KING: We have seen His star in the East. We have followed it to your city.

THIRD KING: Yes, we have come to adore Him. Is He in your palace?

HEROD: Great Kings, find the newborn King. Come back to tell me where He is. I, too, want to adore Him.

KINGS: We thank you, great Herod. We will do so. (*They leave the palace.*)

HEROD (*walks about the room in great anger*): I am King of the Jews. I will kill that newborn King when I find Him!

Scene III. In the Stable

(*The star has stopped above the stable. The Kings get down from their camels.*)

FIRST KING: The star stops above the stable. Here must be the King of the Jews.

SECOND KING: Come, let us adore Him because He is the great God!

THIRD KING (*raising his hands to heaven*): God of Heaven and Earth, we thank Thee. (*They go into the stable and find Jesus, Mary, and Joseph.*)

ALL (*kneeling before Jesus*): Savior of the World! We adore Thee!

(*The Infant Jesus blesses them.*)

Scene IV. At Night

(*An Angel appears to the Kings in a dream.*)

ANGEL: Great Kings of the East! Do not go back to Herod because he will kill the Infant. I will show you another way home.

(*The Angel goes back to heaven. The Kings wake up.*)

FIRST KING: An angel appeared to me in my dream.

SECOND KING: An angel appeared to me, too. He said we should not go back to Herod because he will kill the Baby Jesus.

THIRD KING: The angel said he would show us some other way home.

ALL (*kneel*): We thank Thee, great God. We will obey. (*They return to the East by some other way.*)

SOMETHING TO DRAW

Draw a star such as you think the Magi saw.

Draw a camel such as you think the Magi rode.

JOSEPH AND MARY TOOK JESUS TO FAR-AWAY EGYPT

8. A CRUEL KING

Herod was very angry. This story tells you how cruel he was and what happened to Baby Jesus.

* * *

St. Joseph was sleeping.

An angel of the Lord appeared to him in his dreams.

"Arise, take the Child and His Mother and go into Egypt! Stay there until I shall tell you. Herod will seek the Child to kill Him," said the angel.

At once Joseph told Mary. She dressed Baby Jesus quickly, and soon they were on their journey to far-away Egypt.

No! Herod could never kill the Savior Jesus.

But what did King Herod do? Oh, he was a very cruel king. He sent many soldiers to Bethlehem to kill all the little baby boys. He was sure the Infant Jesus would be killed, too.

But Baby Jesus was far, far away, going to Egypt.

After some years the cruel Herod died.

The angel appeared again to St. Joseph in a dream in far-away Egypt.

"Arise, take the Child and His Mother and go back to the land of Israel!" were the happy words of the angel.

Joseph, Mary, and Jesus obeyed the word of God.

They went back home to the country of Israel and lived in Nazareth.

How happy the Holy Family was in Nazareth!

DO YOU KNOW

1. Who said these words?
2. When were they said?

    Hail, Mary, full of grace.
    Behold the Handmaid of the Lord.
    This day is born to you a Savior.
    Glory to God in the highest.
    Arise, take the Child and His Mother.
    We have seen His star in the East.
    I, too, will adore Him.

9. TO A LITTLE BOY

Jesus lived with His parents in Nazareth. This poem tells about the many things Jesus did. Ask Jesus to be your Leader.

* * *

When Jesus was a little boy like you,
The things that He would do!
He'd sweep the floor
And tidy up the room,
While Mary sat before the door,
A-spinning at her loom.
Then off to play He'd happily go,
Or off to Joseph's shop.
The merriest boy you'd care to know.
Skip, skip, hippity-hop!
He loved the folk of Nazareth-town,
And they all loved Him, too!
But do you know whom He loved best?
A little boy like YOU!

—*C. A. Burns, S.J.*

WHAT I WILL DO FOR LOVE OF JESUS
I will help mother in the house today. How?
I will help my father some way today. How?
I will have a happy smile for everyone today.
I will do my work for Jesus today.

10. A MOTHER'S QUEST

When Jesus was twelve years old, His parents took Him to the Temple in Jerusalem. There Jesus was lost. The poem tells you about the great sorrow of His Mother.

* * *

Have you seen my little Love
   Going by your door?
Off He flew, my little Dove,
   And my heart is sore.
You would know my little Boy,
   Dressed in white and brown.
How my heart o'erflowed with joy
   As I wove His gown.
Oh, if you should see my Own,
   Seeking out His home,

Tell Him how my joy has flown
   As the streets I roam.
And if hungry He should be,
   Give Him of your bread!
If He nod so wearily,
   Make His little bed.
Woman, if you see my Boy,
   Oh, to Him be kind!
You will have the fullest joy—
   Lo! 'Tis God you'll find.

—*Rev. H. F. Blunt*

SOMETHING TO DO

Tell what you would have done for the lost Jesus.

Tell what Mary asked anyone to do for her lost Boy.

JESUS IN THE TEMPLE

11. JESUS IN THE TEMPLE

In the poem you saw how sad Mother Mary was because Jesus was lost to her. This story tells you how she and St. Joseph found Him.

* * *

For three days Joseph and Mary looked for their lost Boy among friends. Not finding Him, they returned to Jerusalem.

They walked back to the Temple of God where they had prayed with Jesus. Surely He must be here in the House of His Father.

Suddenly they heard the sweet voice of Jesus. They found Him in the Temple, sitting among the teachers, hearing them and asking them many things.

Mother Mary and St. Joseph listened. Jesus, the twelve-year-old Boy, was speaking holy and wise words to these teachers in the Temple. They all heard with great joy the wonderful words of this wonderful Boy.

When Jesus had stopped speaking, His Mother and St. Joseph walked toward Him.

His Mother said to Him: "Son, why hast Thou done so to us? Thy father and I have looked for Thee with sorrow."

Jesus loved His holy Mother and said kindly to her: "Mother, why didst thou look for Me? Didst thou not know that I must be about My Father's business?"

He went back with them to Nazareth. There He lived for many years and obeyed Mary, His Mother, and Joseph, His foster father.

And Jesus advanced in wisdom, and age, and grace with God and men.

SOMETHING TO DO

Show your little brother the picture in your book. Tell him how Jesus was lost and found.

12. JESUS SAYS GOOD-BY

Do you remember the Loving Promise God made to Adam and Eve? This story tells you how Jesus was now ready to keep God's promise.

* * *

Jesus, the Son of God and the Son of Mary, was thirty years old.

One morning Jesus and His dear Mother Mary stood before their home in Nazareth. They were saying good-by because Jesus was going away. He would now teach the people the way to God.

Soon Jesus would open the gates of heaven again. But, oh, He would suffer so very, very much. He would die on a cruel cross.

Mary knew all this, but she said to Jesus: "My sweet Son, go. Save the poor children of

earth. I, too, will suffer for them. I will pray for them."

Jesus blessed His holy Mother and held her to His heart.

"Good-by, My Mother," Jesus said, and then He went away.

Jesus left His home to save all men.

ANSWER THESE QUESTIONS

How do I show my mother that I love her?

Do I always obey her?

Am I always happy to obey her?

Did I pray for her today?

Do I ask mother if I may help her with the work?

Do I often thank God for my good mother?

What will I do for her today?

A GAME

Ask your little friend these questions. Let him ask you, too.

Who won the game? Play it with your father.

Whom did God promise to send to earth to save men?

Who is the Father of Jesus?

Who is the foster father of Jesus?
Who is the Mother of Jesus?
Who is St. Joseph?
Is Jesus true God?
Is Jesus true man?
Where was Jesus born?
When was Jesus born?
To whom did the angels tell the story of Jesus?
To whom did a star show the way to Jesus?
Who was a very wicked king?
What did he want to do?
Where did the Holy Family go?
After some years, where did they return?
How old was Jesus when He was lost?
Where was He lost?
Where was He found?
Whom did Jesus obey?
How did Jesus advance?
How old was Jesus when He said good-by to His Mother?
Why did Jesus go away from home?

JESUS BEGINS HIS PUBLIC LIFE

PART III. THE FIRST STORIES OF JESUS' PUBLIC LIFE

1. JESUS AND ST. JOHN

Jesus had said good-by to His Mother. He went to the River Jordan. This story tells you about a wonderful thing that happened here.

* * *

Many, many people had come to the River Jordan.

John, the son of Elizabeth, was telling them about the Savior of the world.

Suddenly John stopped speaking because he saw Jesus coming toward him.

"Behold the Lamb of God who taketh away the sins of the world," John cried out to the people.

They all looked at Jesus. Perhaps it was the first time they saw Jesus, the Son of God.

Jesus came to John to be baptized by him in the River Jordan.

ST. JOHN BAPTIZING JESUS

John cried out to the Lord: "I ought to be baptized by Thee!"

Jesus said to him: "Let it be so now!" And John baptized Jesus.

Behold Heaven was opened, and the Holy Ghost came down upon Jesus in the form of a dove. The voice of God the Father came from the clouds saying: "This is My Son!"

>God the Father,
>God the Son,
>God the Holy Ghost,
>Be praised forever!

Holy Trinity, One God! Be praised forever!

SOMETHING TO ANSWER

Is the Father God?
Is the Son God?
Is the Holy Ghost God?
Is there but one God?
How many persons are there in God?

2. JESUS IN THE DESERT

The devil tries to make people sin. He even tried three times to make Jesus sin. The story tells you what Jesus did to the devil.

* * *

After Jesus had been baptized by St. John, He went to the desert all alone to pray.

For forty days and nights, Jesus prayed for the world. He prayed for me, too.

During all these days, Jesus did not eat anything. At last He became very, very hungry.

The devil came into the desert. He wanted to make Jesus sin, as he had made Adam and Eve sin.

"If Thou be the Son of God, command that these stones be made bread," the devil said to Jesus.

Jesus answered him: "Not in bread alone does man live, but by every word of God."

Jesus wanted to show us that it is better to be hungry than to sin. Nothing in the world is so bad as sin.

Again the devil tried to tempt Jesus to sin.

He took Jesus high upon the temple. He told Jesus to cast Himself down to the street below, for it was promised that the angels of God would care for Him.

Jesus said: "Thou shalt not tempt the Lord thy God!"

Jesus wanted to teach us that to be proud is a sin.

* * *

Once more the devil tempted Jesus.

He took the Savior onto a very high mountain and showed Him the big, beautiful world.

"All this will I give Thee if Thou wilt adore me," the devil said.

In holy anger Jesus cried out to him: "Go away, Satan! The Lord thy God shalt thou adore. Him alone shalt thou serve."

Then the devil left Jesus.

Behold! Angels came from heaven to serve Jesus.

Jesus wanted to teach us that we must never do what is a sin, not even for everything in the world.

WHAT WOULD YOU DO?

You see some fruit. It is not yours. The devil says: "Take it. No one will see you." The devil is tempting you. What should you do? Can you tell of other times when the devil tempts children?

3. THE APOSTLES ARE CHOSEN

Jesus came to save the people of the world. He wanted some men to help Him. This story tells you about these men. Would you like to help Jesus in this holy work?

* * *

Jesus left the desert. He passed through cities and towns, teaching the people about God. Jesus wanted some good men to help Him in this great work.

One morning Jesus was at the sea. Hard-working men were trying to catch some fish.

Suddenly a little boat came near. Two men in the boat were pulling in their nets. Jesus looked kindly at these men.

"Come!" He said to the men. "I will make you fishers of men."

The two men looked into the sweet face of God. At once they left all and followed Jesus.

One of these men was Andrew. He went at once to find his brother Simon to tell him what had happened. Simon, whom we know as Peter, became an Apostle, too.

On the same day Jesus, Peter, and Andrew were again at the seaside.

An old man sat in his boat getting his net ready for the next morning's fishing. James and John, his two sons, were helping him.

Suddenly they heard their names called. They looked up from their work. The sweet voice of Jesus called them. They, too, looked into the eyes of God and at once followed Jesus.

Now Jesus had four Apostles.

Soon Jesus called Philip, Bartholomew, Thomas, Matthew, another James, Thaddeus, Simon, and Judas.

These twelve men were the Twelve Apostles of Jesus.

They were all happy to help Jesus teach men the way to heaven.

SOMETHING TO DRAW

Draw any picture you see in this story.

Why would you draw a lake, a ship, some fish in the lake, fishermen in the ship?

4. THE FIRST MIRACLE OF JESUS

A miracle is such a wonderful thing that only God can work it. This story tells you about the first miracle of Jesus.

* * *

There was a wedding in Cana. Mother Mary, Jesus, and His Apostles went to the wedding.

Everything was ready. There was sweet music and everyone was happy. The wedding people stood before Jesus because they wanted Him to bless them. He blessed them and made them happy.

Soon the dinner was ready. What a wonderful wedding this was because Jesus and Mary were there.

But, oh, after a little time, something happened! There was no more wine!

Mother Mary said to Jesus: "They have no wine."

Jesus looked kindly at His Mother and said: "Woman, what is that to Me and to thee? My hour is not yet come."

Mary knew Jesus would help the wedding people. She said to the waiters: "Do what He shall say!"

Now there were six large waterpots standing near the door. Jesus said to the waiters: "Fill the waterpots with water."

They filled them all.

Then Jesus said to the waiters: "Carry some to the chief steward." They obeyed Jesus.

The chief steward tasted it. It was not water any more, but the best wine! Jesus had changed the water to wine!

This was the first great miracle of Jesus.

ANSWER YES OR NO

Jesus went to a wedding.

This was a happy wedding.

Mother Mary was not at the wedding.

The Apostles were at the wedding.

They had enough wine.

Jesus changed water into wine.

This wine was not good.

This was the first great miracle of Jesus.

REVIEW TEST

Who said these words? When were they said?

This is My Son.

Go away, Satan! The Lord thy God shalt thou adore.

I will make you fishers of men.

Do what He shall say!

Find the pictures that tell the stories of these words.

Tell the class the story of one picture.

PART IV. THE MOST WONDERFUL STORY EVER TOLD

1. THE SERVANT OF A CENTURION

Jesus showed by His miracles that He is God. This is a story about a very sick servant. Read what Jesus did for him.

* * *

Capharnaum was a beautiful city near the sea.

Jesus loved to be in Capharnaum. It was here that He worked many miracles.

One day Jesus was again in Capharnaum.

Just at this time the servant of a centurion became very sick. Not even the best doctors could save his life.

Now the centurion, an officer in the army, loved his sick servant very much. He was very, very sad. What could he do to save the life of his servant?

"I will go to Jesus, the great Master. He will help my servant," he said. At once he was on his way to Jesus.

"Lord," the centurion said when he found Jesus, "my servant is at home very sick." And he knelt at the feet of the Lord.

Jesus answered him: "I will come and heal him."

Oh, the great joy of the centurion! He knew Jesus was God.

"Lord," he cried to Jesus, "I am not worthy that Thou shouldst come under my roof. Say only the word, and my servant shall be healed."

And the Lord said to him: "Go. As thou hast believed, so be it done!"

A great miracle happened. At these words of Jesus, the sick servant was healed. Rising from his bed, he cried: "I am healed! I am healed!"

When the centurion came home, he found his servant healed.

The centurion and all his family believed in Jesus.

SOMETHING TO WRITE

Write sentences with the words: servant, sick, heal, worthy, miracle, centurion.

2. JESUS AND A CRIPPLED MAN

This story is about a poor, crippled man. Jesus did two wonderful things for him. Can you find what they were?

* * *

Jesus was in the house of a good friend in Capharnaum.

Crowds of people soon filled the house and the yard to see and to hear the great Master.

Jesus was teaching them wonderful things about God.

Suddenly something happened in the yard. Four men were bringing a poor, crippled man on his bed to Jesus. They tried hard to get through the crowds, but they could not get near to Jesus.

"I know what we can do," said one of the men. "Let us take him up to the roof. We can open the roof and let down the bed before Jesus."

Was not that a fine plan?

Soon they were safe on the roof and began

JESUS HEALS THE CRIPPLED MAN

to open it. They put ropes around the bed.

Easily, quietly, the bed came down from the roof—down before the Lord.

Oh, the joy in the heart of Jesus!

Oh, the surprise of the people!

Jesus said to the crippled man: "Son, thy sins are forgiven thee."

Some people thought: "Who can forgive sins but God?"

Jesus knew what they were thinking. He said to them: "That you may know that the Son of Man can forgive sins, I say: 'Arise! Take thy bed and go into thy house!'"

At once the crippled man rose, and kneeling, he thanked Jesus. Then he took up his bed and walked home!

Jesus had healed the soul of this man from sin. He had also healed his crippled body.

When the people saw this miracle, they all praised God.

SOMETHING TO WRITE

Write some ways in which you can be kind to the poor or to the sick.

3. JESUS AND A BLIND MAN

How good Jesus was to all the sick people. You will like the story of Jesus and the blind man very much.

* * *

Every day a poor, blind man sat by the wayside near the city of Jericho, asking for help.

One day Jesus and many people were coming down the road from Jericho. The crowds were singing and praising God.

"Please!" cried out the blind man, "please, tell me why so many people are coming from Jericho?"

A kind man answered him: "Jesus of Nazareth is passing by."

"Jesus! Jesus! Have mercy on me!" the blind man cried.

Suddenly Jesus stood still. All became very, very quiet.

Soon the blind man was kneeling at the feet of Jesus.

"What wilt thou that I do for thee?" asked

the sweetest voice the blind man had ever heard.

"Lord, that I may see!" he asked, as he lifted his blind eyes to the face of Jesus.

Jesus said to him: "Go thy way! Thy faith hath made thee whole."

The eyes of the blind man opened wide! He looked into the holy eyes of his God.

And he followed Jesus ever after.

WHAT CAN I DO WITH MY EYES FOR JESUS?

When I see something beautiful?
When I see something bad?
When I am in church?
When I am in school?
When I take care of the baby?
What else can I do with my eyes for Jesus?

DO YOU KNOW

What is faith?
What is hope?
What is love?
How did this blind man show faith, hope, and love?

4. JESUS AND THE LEPERS

A Play

TIME: When Jesus lived.

CHARACTERS: Jesus, Ten Lepers, People.

Scene I. Among the Lepers

(*The lepers are walking among the rocks and caves. They are sad.*)

FIRST LEPER: My friends, here we are poor, alone, covered with sores. There will be no more happy life for us. I wish I could die!

SECOND LEPER: What are you saying? Do you not know that God takes care of us, too?

THIRD LEPER: I have heard about a great Man, Jesus of Nazareth. He makes the blind to see, the lame to walk. They say He helps lepers, too. I think He must be the Savior.

(*A large crowd of people, coming down the road, is singing*: "*Hail to Jesus of Nazareth!*")

FOURTH LEPER: Do you hear what they are singing? Jesus of Nazareth is passing by!

ALL LEPERS: Oh, come, let us go to Him. He will heal us.

(*The people, seeing the lepers, cry out in fear and run away.*)

ALL LEPERS: Jesus, Master, have mercy on us!

JESUS (*raising His hands to them*): Go! Show yourselves to the priests!

Scene II. On the Road to Jerusalem

(*The lepers are hurrying to the city to show themselves to the priests.*)

EIGHTH LEPER: Thanks be to God! See, my sores are healing.

NINTH LEPER: Oh, look! My face, my hands! Clean! Clean!

TENTH LEPER: Let us go faster. Jesus is the Savior!

Scene III. On the Road

(*The lepers are all healed.*)

THIRD LEPER: Friends, let us go back to thank Jesus.

FIRST LEPER: I am going home.

ALL LEPERS: I want to see my family first. I will thank Him some other time. I am healed. I do not care to go back.

(*All hurry away. Only one goes back to Jesus.*)

Scene IV.   At the Feet of Jesus

THIRD LEPER: Oh, I thank Thee, my God.

JESUS (*sadly*): Were not ten made clean? Where are the other nine? (*Kindly to the good leper*): Go thy way, thy faith hath made thee whole.

(*The leper goes home happy.*)

ANSWER THESE QUESTIONS

Where were the lepers?
How many lepers were there?
Who was coming down the road?
What did the lepers do?
What did they ask Jesus?
What did Jesus do for them?
How many lepers came back to thank Jesus?
Why was Jesus sad?
Do you thank Jesus often?

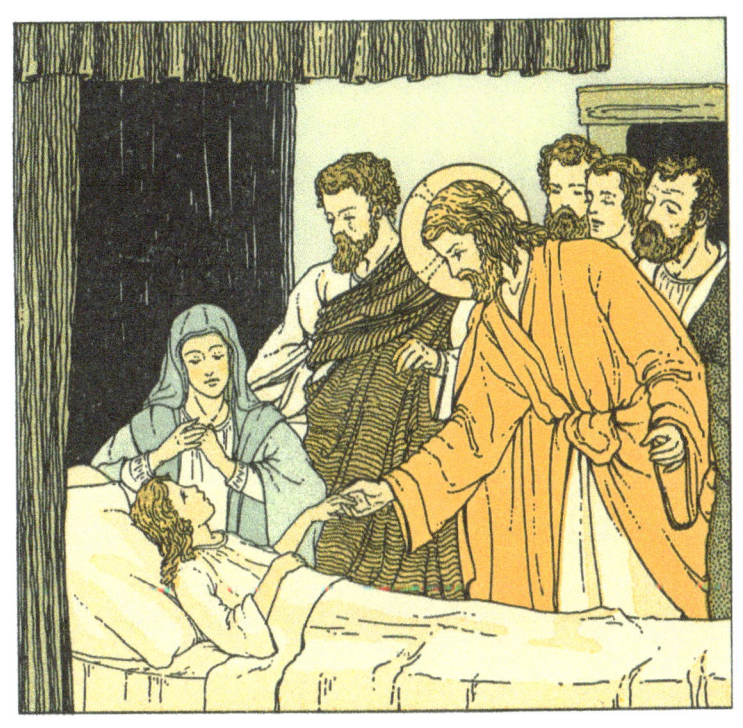

5. THE DAUGHTER OF JAIRUS

The story tells you something wonderful Jesus did for a little girl twelve years old.

* * *

A long, long time ago, a happy girl lived with her father Jairus and her mother. Her parents loved their sweet daughter very much.

One day this happy child became sick.

The doctors said to Jairus: "We cannot heal your daughter. She must die."

The heart of Jairus was so sad! The dear mother prayed and prayed.

"God will save our only child," Jairus cried. "I will go to Jesus."

Soon Jairus was kneeling before Jesus.

"Lord!" he prayed, "my little daughter is sick. Come, lay Thy hand upon her and she will live."

Jesus and Jairus started at once on their way to the sick girl.

Suddenly they saw a servant running down the street toward them. He stopped before Jairus and cried out: "Thy daughter is dead!"

The poor, poor father!

Jesus whispered to him: "Fear not! Believe and she shall be safe."

When they came to the home, they saw the people weeping.

Jesus said to them: "Weep not! The girl is not dead, but only sleeps."

And they laughed at Him!

Jesus commanded all the people to leave the room. Only her own parents, and Peter, James, and John, were with Jesus at the bed of the dead child.

Jesus took the little hand of the girl into His holy hand.

"Maid, arise!" He said, and she rose from the dead!

Jesus put her into the arms of her happy parents.

What a grand miracle! Only God can raise the dead to life!

FILL IN THE SPACES

This little girl was the daughter of ....

She became very ....

Her father went to .... for help.

Jairus asked Jesus to .... his daughter.

The servant said: Thy daughter is ....

Jesus said to the father: ....

Jesus said: The girl is not .... but only ....

And the child .... from the dead.

This was a grand ....

6. THE ONLY SON OF HIS MOTHER

This story is about Jesus, a poor old mother, and her only son. Read it to your big brother or your father or mother at home.

* * *

One evening Jesus and His Apostles were going to a little city called Naim. They had just come to the gates of the city.

See! A sad crowd of people was leaving Naim. Jesus and all His friends stopped to let them pass.

Four men were carrying the dead son of a poor old mother out of the city. All alone, the sad mother walked just behind the body of her only son.

The poor, poor mother!

When Jesus saw her, His sweet heart became sad. Going to the weeping mother, Jesus said to her: "Weep not!"

She raised her eyes and looked into the kind face of Jesus. What joy He brought into her poor, sad heart by His loving words.

JESUS RAISES THE WIDOW'S SON FROM THE DEAD

Jesus, commanding all to stop, walked close to the dead man. Everyone watched the Lord. What was He going to do?

For a moment Jesus looked at the dead man. All stood still, very still!

"Young man, I say to thee, arise!" were the words of Jesus.

At once the young man rose from the dead! And Jesus gave him back to his old mother.

The people were filled with joy and with fear. They praised God.

CAN YOU ANSWER THESE QUESTIONS?

Who gave you life?

Who gives everyone life?

Will your body die?

Will your soul die?

How can you make your soul very pleasing to God?

What should you do when you have sinned?

Must you take care of your body?

Why do you think so?

Must you take more care of your soul or of your body? Why?

7. SOME DEAR FRIENDS OF JESUS

Jesus had some very dear friends. This story is about them.

* * *

About a mile from Jerusalem was a little town called Bethany. In a beautiful house of Bethany, Lazarus, Martha, and Mary, three dear friends of Jesus, lived in great joy and love.

Jesus loved to visit Bethany.

Lazarus, the brother of Martha and Mary, was a holy man.

Martha was always so busy, keeping the house beautiful. She loved to do this for her dear ones and for Jesus.

Mary loved best of all just to think of Jesus.

Jesus loved them all, but He loved Mary best. Once upon a time Mary had been a sinner. Jesus had changed her into a saint.

When Jesus came to Bethany, Mary sat at His feet and listened to His holy words.

One day Mary was again at the feet of her Lord. Martha was busy with the dinner and she wanted Mary to help her.

Martha said to Jesus: "Lord, speak to my sister that she help me."

But Jesus said: "Martha! Martha! Thou art busy about many things. Only one thing is necessary. Mary has chosen the better part."

SOMETHING TO WRITE

Write sentences with these words in them: Jesus, Bethany, Lazarus, Martha, Mary, Saint, I.

8. JESUS AND LAZARUS

A Play

TIME: When Jesus lived.

CHARACTERS: Jesus, Lazarus, Martha, Mary, Apostles, People.

Scene I. In Bethany near Jerusalem

(*Lazarus is very sick. Mary and Martha are with him.*)

MARY: If only the Lord Jesus were here, He would help us.

LAZARUS: Fear not, my dear sisters, He will come.

MARTHA: I shall send a message to Him. It will be: Lord, he whom Thou lovest is sick. (*She calls a servant and gives him the message. He hurries to Jesus, who is far, far away.*)

Scene II. Far from Bethany

(*Jesus has gone far away from Bethany because His enemies in Jerusalem want to kill Him. The servant has come to Jesus.*)

SERVANT (*kneeling before Jesus*): Lord, I bring a message from Bethany: He whom

Thou lovest is sick. (*The servant returns home.*)

JESUS (*to His Apostles*): Lazarus, our friend, has been very sick. He is sleeping.

APOSTLE: Lord, if he is sleeping, he shall do well.

JESUS (*sadly*): Lazarus is dead! Let us go to him.

THOMAS (*bravely*): Let us go also that we may die with Jesus.

(*They start for Bethany near Jerusalem.*)

Scene III. Near Bethany

(*Jesus and His Apostles have come.*)

MARTHA (*meeting them on the road*): Lord, if Thou hadst been here, my brother would not have died.

JESUS (*kindly*): Thy brother shall rise again.

MARTHA: I know that he shall rise again on the last day.

JESUS: Everyone that believeth in Me shall not die forever.

MARTHA: Lord, I believe that Thou art Christ, the Son of the Living God. (*Martha calls Mary to Jesus.*)

MARY (*kneeling before Jesus*): Lord, if Thou hadst been here, my brother would not have died.

JESUS: Where have you laid him?

MARY: Lord, come and see.

(*Mary takes Jesus to the tomb, and many people follow them.*)

Scene IV. At the Tomb of Lazarus

(*Jesus weeps.*)

PEOPLE (*seeing Jesus weep*): See, how He loved him.

JESUS (*standing at the tomb*): Take away the stone!

MARTHA: Lord, he is dead four days. (*Men take away the stone. The dead body of Lazarus is all bound up with white cloth.*)

JESUS (*lifting His eyes to heaven, prays*): Father, I give Thee thanks. (*In a loud voice*): Lazarus, come forth! (*And Lazarus comes from the tomb!*)

JESUS: Loose him, and let him go.

(*They loose him. All are filled with fear.*)

LAZARUS, MARY, MARTHA (*kneeling before Jesus*): O God, we thank Thee!

(*Jesus and His Apostles go home with Lazarus to Bethany.*)

ANSWER YES OR NO

Did Jesus love Lazarus?

Did Jesus know before the servant came that Lazarus was dead?

Did Jesus tell the Apostles about Lazarus?

Did Jesus go to Bethany?

Did Jesus go to the tomb of Lazarus?

Did Jesus tell Lazarus to stay in the tomb?

Could Jesus work this miracle because He is God?

REVIEW TESTS

Find a picture that tells about these words. Tell the story of the picture.

Maid, arise!

Lord, my servant is at home sick unto death.

Arise, take up thy bed and go into thy house.

Were not ten made clean? Where are the other nine?

Lord, that I may see.

Young man, I say to thee, Arise!

Lazarus, come forth!

JESUS HELPS THE APOSTLES CATCH FISH

PART V. STORIES OF THE SEA

1. A WONDERFUL FISHING TRIP

You have learned how Jesus healed the sick and raised the dead. The next stories tell you of some other great miracles.

* * *

Early one morning Jesus was again on the seashore. People had come to listen to His holy words.

Jesus stepped into Peter's boat and spoke to them.

After Jesus had said many beautiful things, He and His Apostles sailed over the bright, blue sea.

When they were out in the deep waters, Jesus said to Peter: "Let down your net into the water."

"Master," Peter answered Jesus, "we have worked all the night and have caught nothing. But at Thy word, I will let down the net."

He did so.

Oh, the surprise! In a moment hundreds of fish filled the net. There were so many fish that the net broke.

"Help! Help!" Peter cried to the Apostles in another boat.

Soon both boats were so filled with fish that they nearly sank.

Peter knelt at the feet of Jesus and said: "Depart from me, O Lord, for I am a sinful man."

But Jesus said to him: "Fear not, Peter. From now on thou shalt catch men."

FIND THE RIGHT ENDING

Jesus was preaching { on the mountain. / on the seashore. / in a city.

Jesus was in { the boat of Peter. / the boat of James. / the boat of John.

In the night they caught { a few fish. / nothing. / hundreds of fish.

In the morning they caught { nothing. / a few fish. / hundreds of fish.

Jesus said, { Help, Help! / Master, we have worked all the night. / Fear not, Peter.

2. A STORM ON THE SEA

This story tells you about a wonderful thing Jesus did during a storm. Tell your father the story.

* * *

Evening came and Jesus was tired. He stepped into Peter's boat again.

"Let us go to the other side of the sea," He said to Peter.

Soon the ship was sailing over the beautiful, blue sea. Jesus lay in the boat, sleeping.

All was quiet, so quiet. The Apostles tried hard not to wake Jesus.

Suddenly a terrible storm came down upon the sea. The sky became black.

JESUS CALMS THE SEA

The waves grew higher and higher. The winds almost blew them all into the sea.

Jesus was still sleeping.

At last the Apostles called Him.

"Lord, save us!" they cried out in great fear.

Jesus, rising, held out His arms over the black waves. He commanded them: "Peace, be still!"

And the winds stopped.... And the waves became quiet.... All was still, very still....

Oh, how great is the Lord Jesus! He is the Master of the winds and of the seas.

The Apostles were filled with fear. Jesus said to them: "Why are you afraid?"

All in the boat said: "What manner of Man is this? Even the winds and the sea obey Him."

And then they knew that God stood in the boat with them.

SOMETHING TO DO

Draw any part of the story you like.

Tell your little brother about the storm at sea.

3. ANOTHER WONDERFUL SEA STORY

Jesus shows again that He is God. Which part of the story do you like best?

* * *

It was very late at night. Peter's boat was again sailing over the sea, but this time Jesus was not with Peter. He was praying on the mountain.

Suddenly a terrible storm came down upon them again! The waves dashed against the boat. The winds were wild and the sea black. The sails on the boat were torn by the storm.

Surely this time all would be lost. Oh, if Jesus were only in the boat!

See! Something white was walking over the water! It drew nearer and nearer!

"A ghost!" shouted someone.

It was walking on the wild water toward them.

"Be of good heart, it is I. Fear ye not!" said the sweet voice of Jesus.

JESUS WALKS ON THE WATERS

Jesus was walking over the water, coming to help His poor Apostles.

"Lord," cried Peter, "if it is Thou, tell me to come to Thee upon the water."

"Come!" said Jesus, and Peter jumped out of his boat and walked on the water toward Jesus.

As he was walking on the sea, the wind grew wild again. A big wave came toward Peter.

"Lord, save me!" he cried, and he began to sink.

Jesus took Peter by the hand. On the water they walked back to the boat.

At once the storm stopped. All in the boat adored Jesus and said: "Thou art the Son of God."

A GAME

Ask your little friend some questions about this story.

Let him ask you some questions.

Who won the game?

Play this game with your father and mother.

REVIEW ON MIRACLES

Match the story with the miracle.

Story About

a wedding in Cana

a Centurion

a man on the way to Jericho

nine men who did not thank Jesus

a little girl

the only son of his mother

a man who had been four days in the tomb

a fishing trip

a storm on the lake

Miracle

a servant healed

a young man raised from the dead

Lazarus raised from the dead

hundreds of fish caught

water changed to wine

a blind man sees

ten lepers healed

a wild sea is stilled at once

a little girl raised from the dead

PART VI. JESUS' STORY HOUR

THE GOOD SHEPHERD

I am the Good Shepherd.

The Good Shepherd gives His life for His sheep.

I lay down My life for My sheep.

I know Mine, and Mine know Me.

And other sheep I have. They are not of this fold.

I must also bring them.

They shall hear My voice.

There shall be one fold and one Shepherd.

SOMETHING TO DO

Think about these beautiful words of Jesus.

1. THE LOST SHEEP

Jesus told this story to the people. Find out who the Good Shepherd is. Who is the Lost Sheep?

* * *

Once upon a time there lived a good, kind shepherd. He loved his sheep and his sheep loved him. He always brought the sheep and their little lambs into the richest pastures.

At night the shepherd brought them back home to the fold. He often carried the tired little lambs in his arms.

One day a little lamb ran away, far, far away. He thought he was so happy. Now he could see the big, beautiful world. He was free, free!

All day long he ran and played in the pastures.

Soon night came. It was very, very dark. The wolves began to come nearer and nearer. The little runaway lamb tried to hide in a bush. There he waited all alone.

JESUS, THE GOOD SHEPHERD

Oh, why had he been so bad? Why had he not stayed home with his kind shepherd?

Far, far away the good shepherd was counting his sheep.

"Oh, where is my little lamb? Where can he be?" cried the shepherd. "I must find him and bring him home because the wolves may eat him."

The shepherd began to look for the little runaway lamb. He hurried over hills and through pastures.

"Little lamb! My little lamb, where are you?" the shepherd cried.

Suddenly he heard a very little voice.

"That is my lost lamb," he cried with joy.

Soon he found the lamb hiding in the bush and he carried him back home. The good shepherd forgave his little lamb.

He said to his friends: "Be glad with me. I have found my lost sheep."

Which was the happiest little lamb in the fold that night?

SOMETHING TO DO

Draw pictures of the story.

Write a little story. In the story Jesus is the Good Shepherd and you are Jesus' little lamb.

Play the story with your little friends.

2. THE GOOD SAMARITAN

Jesus wanted to teach us how to love our neighbor and so He told us this story.

* * *

One day Jesus was speaking about the love of God and neighbor. Suddenly a lawyer rose and asked Him: "Master, what must I do to go to heaven?"

Jesus said to him: "What is written in the law?"

The man answered: "Thou shalt love the Lord thy God with thy whole heart and with thy whole soul. Thou shalt love thy neighbor as thyself."

Jesus said to him: "Thou hast answered right."

"But who is my neighbor?" asked the lawyer.

Jesus then told this story:

Once upon a time a man went from Jerusalem to Jericho. A band of robbers, hiding in the mountains, saw him. When he came near, the robbers dashed upon him. They took everything he had, wounded him, and ran away.

A Jewish priest, coming down the road, saw the wounded man, but passed on.

A Levite came. He also saw the wounded man, and passed on.

At last a good man, a Samaritan, passed the same way. He saw the wounded man and was filled with pity for him. He bound up his wounds, and putting him on his own horse, brought him to an inn.

The Samaritan said to the master of the inn: "Here is some money. Take good care of this wounded man. I will pay for all he needs."

Then Jesus asked the lawyer: "Which of these men was a neighbor to the wounded man?"

"He that showed mercy to him," the man answered.

And Jesus said: "Go, and do in like manner."

SOMETHING TO DO

Make a booklet called "My Neighbor."

Find pictures of little children who live in different parts of the world. They are all your neighbors.

Paste these pictures in your booklet.

Tell how you can show mercy to your neighbor.

3. THE PHARISEE AND THE PUBLICAN

A Play

TIME: When Jesus lived.
CHARACTERS: Pharisee, Publican.
PLACE: The Temple of Jerusalem.

(*Two men went up to the Temple to pray. One was a Pharisee and the other a Publican.*)

PHARISEE (*dressed in rich silks, walks*

proudly through the Temple. He prays so all can see and hear him):

O God, I give Thee thanks that I am not as the rest of men. (*He points to the Publican.*) I thank Thee that I am not like this Publican. I give much money to the Temple.

(*The Pharisee walks proudly out of the Temple. God was not pleased with his prayer.*)

PUBLICAN (*dressed in poor clothes. He stands where no one can see or hear him*): O God, have mercy on me, a sinner!

(*The Publican leaves the Temple. God was pleased with his prayer.*)

ANSWER THESE QUESTIONS

Which of these men do you like better?

Why do you like him better?

Why did God not hear the prayers of the Pharisee?

Why did God hear the prayer of the Publican?

When will God be pleased with your prayer?

Why must you pray to God?

When does a good child pray?

For whom should you pray?

4. THE RICH MAN AND LAZARUS

Jesus always told wonderful stories. This day the story was about a rich man and a poor man.

* * *

Once upon a time there was a very rich man. He wore the most beautiful clothes and always had the best of foods.

There was also a very poor man named Lazarus. He often sat at the gate of the rich man's house. If only he could have the little pieces of bread that fell from the rich man's table! But no one gave him any.

One day the rich man died. In life he had not been kind to the poor, and so his soul went to hell.

Lazarus, the poor man, died, too. He had been a very good man and had suffered much for the love of God. Lazarus was carried to heaven.

The rich man looked up from hell and saw

Lazarus happy in heaven, in the bosom of Abraham.

"Oh, if Lazarus would only give me a drink of water," he thought.

Then he cried out: "Oh, Father Abraham, have mercy on me. Please send Lazarus to me. Let him put his finger into water and touch my tongue with it."

Father Abraham said: "Son, you had good things in your life; Lazarus did not. Now Lazarus is happy forever, and you will never be happy!"

SOMETHING TO WRITE

Write sentences about each: priest, commandment, Jerusalem, Lazarus, Samaritan, neighbor, lawyer, mercy.

ANSWER THESE QUESTIONS

Where do good people go after they die?
Is everybody happy in Heaven?
What will we have in Heaven?
Where do bad people go after they die?
What is Hell?
How long will Heaven and Hell last?

5. THE PRODIGAL SON

This is the most beautiful story Jesus told.

* * *

A PLAY

TIME: When Jesus lived.

CHARACTERS: Father, Prodigal Son, Elder Son, Servants, Strangers.

Scene I. In a Beautiful Country Home

(*A kind old father is seated on the porch. His young son stands near him, dressed in the richest silks.*)

FATHER: My son, I am happy to see you. Come, sit down with me.

SON: Father, I am tired of this country life. I want to see the world. Give me the money that will come to me when you die.

FATHER (*sadly*): Oh, my son, how sad you make me feel. Yes, you may have the money if it is your wish. I will give it to you.

(*Father and son go into the house.*)

Scene II. In a Country Far Away

(*The Prodigal Son has spent all his money.*

He is taking care of pigs so that he may get something to eat. Because he is poor and hungry, all his friends have left him.)

PRODIGAL SON (*sadly*): Oh, I am so hungry. Who will give me something to eat?

STRANGERS: We have nothing. Take care of yourself.

PRODIGAL SON (*thinking*): The servants in my father's house have all they need. Here I am hungry, hungry. (*Jumping up*): I will go home to my good father. I will tell him I am sorry. (*He starts walking on the long journey home.*)

Scene III. In His Father's House

(*The father is standing on the porch, watching for his son's return. Suddenly he sees a poor man coming to the house.*)

FATHER: O, my God, I thank Thee. There comes my poor, poor boy.

(*He runs to meet his son, puts his arms around him, and kisses him.*)

PRODIGAL SON (*kneeling and weeping*): Father, I have sinned against heaven and you.

THE PRODIGAL SON RETURNS TO HIS FATHER'S HOUSE

I am not worthy to be called your son. Make me as a servant in your house.

FATHER (*calling his servants*): Quickly bring the best dress. Put it on my son. Put a ring on his finger and shoes on his feet.

SERVANTS: Yes, sir! (*They obey the father.*)

FATHER: Now kill the best calf. Make merry! My son was dead and is come back to life. He was lost and is found.

(*All make merry.*)

Scene IV. In the Yard

(*The older brother is in the field, working. He hears the music. He comes to the house and calls a servant.*)

ELDER SON: What has happened? Why all this music and joy?

SERVANT: Your brother has come home. Everybody is merry.

(*The older son is so angry that he will not go into the house.*)

FATHER (*coming out to him*): Come into the house, my son. Be merry with us. Your brother has come home.

ELDER SON (*still angry*): I have always obeyed you, but you have never made merry for me.

FATHER (*kindly*): Son, you are always with me. All I have is yours. We must make merry. This day your brother was dead and is come to life again. He was lost and is found.

SOMETHING TO DO

Put a line under the right word in each sentence:

The Prodigal Son felt (happy, sad) when he left home.

He did not like (country, city) life any more.

He wanted to have a (good, hard) time.

He forgot his (father, money).

His friends helped him to (spend, save) his money.

Soon all the money was (lost, spent).

Then the Prodigal had to take care of (horses, pigs).

He was very (happy, hungry).

He went back to his (friends, home).

He asked his father to (give him more money, to forgive him).

His father did (forgive, not forgive) him.

The Prodigal Son was again (sad, happy).

Act out the play with your friends.

A RADIO HOUR

This is the Second Grade Broadcasting Station.

Your announcer is..

The Program for the day will be "Jesus' Story Hour."

The first speaker is..

First Speaker: Story of the Lost Sheep.

The next speaker on the program is..............

Second Speaker: Story of the Rich Man and Lazarus.

The next speaker on the program is................

Third Speaker: Story of the Pharisee and the Publican.

The next number on the program is a play, "The Prodigal Son."

The Father is....................................

The Strangers are..

The Servants are……………………………………
The Prodigal Son is………………………………
The Elder Son is……………………………………
The Program will close with a song by the Second Grade.

This is the Second Grade Broadcasting Station signing off until next Tuesday morning at nine o'clock.

Your announcer was…………………………………

ANSWER THESE QUESTIONS

Will we ever see God?
Where will we see God?
What else will we see there?
What are angels?
Are there any angels on earth?
What do we call these angels?
What does our Guardian Angel do?
Who else is in Heaven?
What does the Blessed Virgin do in Heaven?
What do the Saints do in Heaven?

PART VII. SOME BEAUTIFUL WORDS OF JESUS

1. JESUS BLESSES LITTLE CHILDREN

All children love this story about Jesus. It tells how much Jesus loves little children like you.

* * *

One evening a long, long time ago, Jesus made some little Jewish children very happy.

Many people had come to Jesus. They always loved to hear the beautiful things He told them about God.

Suddenly the voices of happy children were heard calling: "Jesus! Jesus!"

Some good mothers were bringing their children to Jesus.

"Go away!" said the Apostles, "Jesus is too tired to speak to you."

But Jesus smiled at the children because He

loved them. He loves very much all good, holy boys and girls!

He said to the Apostles: "Suffer little children to come to Me, for of such is the kingdom of heaven."

Then Jesus opened wide His arms to the children and said: "Come, My little ones!"

The happy children ran into the arms of Jesus. He held them close to His Heart and blessed them and their mothers.

Jesus loves you just as much as He loved these Jewish children. He says to you too: "My little child, come! I love you!"

What will you tell Jesus?

SOMETHING TO DO

Put a line under the one right word in each sentence:

One (morning, evening) children came to Jesus.

Jesus was telling the people (about God, about the country).

Mothers brought (flowers, their children) to Jesus.

The Apostles said: Jesus (is not tired, is tired).

Jesus said to the children: (Come, go away).

Jesus blessed (the Apostles, the children).

Jesus loves (good, naughty) children.

2. JESUS AND A RICH YOUNG MAN

In this story you will find a loving sentence Jesus says to you. When you have found it, tell Jesus what you would like to do.

* * *

The little children and their mothers had just left Jesus.

A rich young man asked Jesus: "Good Master, what shall I do to go to heaven?"

Jesus said to him: "Keep the commandments!"

He answered the Lord: "I have kept the commandments all my life."

And Jesus smiled upon him because He knew that the soul of this young man was holy.

Jesus wanted his soul to be still more beautiful. He said to the man: "If thou wilt be perfect, go, sell all thou hast and give it to the poor. Then come and follow Me!"

What a loving call from Jesus to the young man.

The young man became very sad. He loved all his things too much. No, he could never give them away.

And so he left Jesus.

Perhaps Jesus will say to you some day: "Come, follow Me!" What will you answer Jesus?

SOMETHING TO WRITE

Write some little things Jesus wants every good child to do for love of Him.

3. A MIRACLE AND A PROMISE

This story tells you of a wonderful miracle and a wonderful promise of Jesus. Thank Jesus often for this great promise.

* * *

One day Jesus and His Apostles went up a mountain. More than five thousand men, women, and children followed them. These good people had been with Jesus for three days and had nothing to eat.

Jesus said to Philip: "I have pity on the people. Where shall we get enough bread for them?"

One of the Apostles said: "A boy here has five loaves and two fishes. What are these among so many people?"

Jesus made these thousands of people sit down on the grass.

Then He did a wonderful thing.

He took the five loaves and the two fishes and, thanking God, He blessed them. He told His Apostles to give all the people some of the bread and fishes.

Think of it! With five loaves and two fishes thousands of people had enough to eat.

After some time Jesus said to the Apostles: "Gather all the pieces that are left."

And they gathered twelve baskets full!

A few days later Jesus gave the people a great promise.

He said to them: "I am the Bread of Life. If any man eat of this Bread, he will live forever. The Bread I will give is My Flesh!"

The Jews said: "How can this man give us His Flesh to eat?"

But Jesus said again: "Unless you eat the Flesh of the Son of Man, you shall not have life in you. I am the Bread that came down from heaven. If any man eat of this Bread, he shall live forever."

This was the great promise of the Blessed Sacrament, the Sacrament which Jesus gave to men the night before He died.

A STORY HOUR

Think of a story about Jesus. Tell it to the class.

4. ZACHEUS

This story tells you about some very kind words Jesus spoke to a stranger. You will like the story very much.

* * *

One day Jesus was walking through the city of Jericho. Many people followed Him.

In the crowds there was a very small man named Zacheus. He tried so hard to see Jesus, but he could not because he was too small. Not even when he stood on his tiptoes could he see Jesus. Zacheus felt very, very sad.

Suddenly he thought of a fine plan. Running before the crowds, Zacheus climbed a tree that he might see Jesus. Jesus was to pass by under the tree.

Soon Zacheus was sitting in the tree. Now he could see Jesus.

Jesus and the people came nearer and nearer. How happy Zacheus was! Yes, that was a fine plan, he could see Jesus very well.

In a moment Jesus was passing the tree. Jesus looked up into the tree at Zacheus. A smile of love was on His holy Face.

"Zacheus," He said kindly, "come down. This day I will stay in thy house!"

Zacheus was so happy, he hardly knew what to do. He came down the tree quickly and Jesus, the great Master, went with him to his home.

"Lord," Zacheus said to Him, "I will give half of all I have to the poor." In this way he wanted to thank Jesus for the wonderful visit.

Jesus said to him: "The Son of Man is come to save that which was lost." Jesus meant that He had come to save the souls of all men.

On this day the soul of Zacheus was made holy and beautiful by Jesus, the Son of God.

* * *

You, too, can have a loving visit with Jesus. He is always waiting for you in His golden home in church. If you visit Him with love, Jesus will make your soul holy and beautiful, too.

Would you like to learn this poem?

IN CHURCH

O! Here I am, dear God,
Kneeling at Your throne,
And I know I am not
Kneeling here alone!
For I know that Angels
All around must be,
With their white wings folded.
With their eyes on me,
God, I know that You are
Here because of me,
And I feel Your nearness,
Though I cannot see . . .
And I kneel and whisper:
"God! I love You so!"
And the Angels pass me
Softly, tippy-toe. . . .

—*Mary Dixon Thayer*

5. JESUS' OWN PRAYER

The holiest prayer in the world came from the heart of Jesus. This story tells you about Jesus' own prayer.

*   *   *

It was a holy time.

Jesus was praying. His eyes were turned to heaven and His face was bright and beautiful. He was speaking to His Father in heaven.

The Apostles were watching their Master pray. They, too, wanted to pray like Jesus.

"Master," they said to Him after His prayer, "teach us how to pray."

Jesus was pleased with His Apostles and He said kindly to them: "When you pray, say:

Our Father who art in heaven,

Hallowed be Thy Name.

Thy Kingdom come.

Thy will be done on earth

As it is in heaven.

Give us this day our daily bread.

And forgive us our trespasses,

As we forgive those who trespass against us.

And lead us not into temptation,
But deliver us from evil. Amen."

ASK YOURSELF

How do I say the Our Father?
Do I say it often every day?
Do I say it when I wake from sleep?
Do I say it when I go to sleep?
Do I say it for my parents often?
Do I thank Jesus for His beautiful prayer?

6. JESUS SPEAKS TO ME

Jesus often thought of me. He said many beautiful words just for me. This lesson tells me some of them.

Come to Me!
Watch and pray.
Love your neighbor.
Give to everyone who asks of you.
Blessed are the clean of heart.
Blessed are the merciful.
Blessed are the peacemakers.
What you do to others, you do to Me.
Follow Me!

SOMETHING TO DO

Talk about the beautiful things Jesus says to you.

REVIEW TESTS

Fill in the spaces with Jesus' own words.

Suffer little children to come to....................

Of such is the .... of heaven.

Come, ...Me.

Give us this day our daily....................

Watch and ....

What you do to others, you do to............

Blessed are the .... of heart.

I am the .... of life.

ANSWER THESE QUESTIONS

When does a little child love Jesus most?

What is sin?

What is a big sin called?

What is a little sin called?

How did Adam and Eve sin?

What is that sin called?

Who never had a sin on her soul?

Was she free from Original Sin?

JESUS ENTERS JERUSALEM

PART VIII. THE SADDEST STORY EVER TOLD

1. HOSANNA!

Would you like to go with Jesus? Think you are with Jesus. Read the story.

* * *

The children of Jerusalem were happy.

The men and women of Jerusalem were happy. Jesus, their Master, was coming back to them.

They went out to meet Jesus, who rode into Jerusalem on a donkey.

"Hosanna! Hosanna!" the children sang to Jesus as they threw flowers to Him. Jesus smiled at His happy children and blessed them.

The men and women waved palms and sang: "Blessed is He that cometh in the name of the Lord!" The Lord Jesus blessed them, too.

All were happy. Even the little donkey

seemed happy, for he was bringing Jesus into Jerusalem.

This day Jesus was truly welcomed as King of the Jews!

The enemies of Jesus saw all this. Now they hated Him more and more! Some day they would kill Him.

Jesus and many of the people went into the Temple. Here He healed the sick and did good to all.

What a happy day this was!

SOMETHING TO DO

Tell what you think Jesus said to the children.

Tell what you would have said to Jesus.

Sing a song to Jesus as the children of Judea did.

ANSWER THESE QUESTIONS

Is Jesus really God and really man?
Is Jesus really a King?
Where is He a King?
Whose King is Jesus?

2. THE TEMPLE OF GOD

The Temple of God must be holy. Read what Jesus did one day. It was early morning.

* * *

The streets of Jerusalem were already filled with people.

The holy days of the Jews, the Paschal Days, were here. Thousands of Jews had come from far and near to adore God in the Temple of Jerusalem.

Jesus and His Apostles were in the Temple, too.

On the Paschal Days the Jews offered sheep and doves to God in the Temple.

There was a big yard just before the Temple where men were selling these sheep and doves. Very much noise filled the yard, even the holy Temple of God.

Jesus saw all this. Suddenly He cried out: "My house shall be called the House of Prayer. You have made it a den of thieves."

Then Jesus threw the money tables over.

He drove the men and their animals out of the Temple. Soon the Temple of God was again a holy place. It was again a House of Prayer.

The blind and the sick came to Jesus in the Temple and He healed them all.

SOMETHING TO DO

What is the holiest place on earth?

Why is it so holy?

What should we do in church?

What should we not do in church?

What should we do when we pass the church?

What can we do to make the house of God beautiful?

3. JUDAS, THE THIEF

Now the sad story of Jesus' life begins. Tell Jesus you love Him so much. It will make Him happy.

* *

How the enemies of Jesus hated Him! If only they could kill Him!

Judas, one of the Apostles, had become a very bad man. He was a thief, and he would do anything for money.

One day a terrible thing happened!

Judas wanted more money. He went to the enemies of Jesus.

"What will you give me if I catch Jesus for you?" he asked them.

"We will give you thirty pieces of silver," they answered. And Judas was willing.

The enemies of Jesus were glad because now they could kill Him.

Cruel Judas! Poor Jesus!

Judas could not have done a more terrible thing. Now Satan was in the black, black soul of Judas. He had a mortal sin on his soul!

* * *

It was the holiest evening the world had ever seen.

Jesus was eating His last supper with the Apostles. On the next day He would die for all men.

While they were at supper, Jesus became sad.

"Amen, I say to you, one of you shall betray Me," Jesus said.

All cried out, even Judas: "Is it I, Lord?"

Jesus whispered to John, "It is he to whom I shall give bread."

And Jesus gave the bread to Judas. Jesus is God. He knew all that the wicked Judas had done. Still He loved Judas. Judas would not listen to his God. He left the room and went out into the dark night. Satan was in his black soul.

SOMETHING TO ASK JESUS FOR

Jesus, help me never to commit a mortal sin.

Jesus, please pity the poor sinner in mortal sin.

Jesus, keep me always close to Thee.

Jesus, keep mother and father close to Thee.

ANSWER THESE QUESTIONS

Who came on earth to free us from sin?

What is a mortal sin?

What is a venial sin?

How can our sins be forgiven?

4. JESUS WASHES THE FEET OF HIS APOSTLES

This story tells you more about the gentle Savior.

* * *

The Last Supper was over. Jesus rose from the table.

He tied a cloth about His body and put some water into a dish.

What was the Master going to do? The Apostles looked at Jesus in surprise.

He began to wash the feet of the Apostles and to dry them with the cloth.

The Apostles did not know what to say.

Jesus came to Peter.

"Lord, dost Thou wash my feet?" cried Peter and moved away.

Jesus said to him: "What I do, thou dost not know now, but thou wilt know."

Peter said: "Thou wilt never wash my feet!"

"If I do not wash thee, thou shalt have no part in Me," said the kind Lord.

At once Peter said: "Lord, wash not only my feet, but also my hands and my head." Never would Peter leave Jesus!

And the sweet Lord Jesus washed the feet of Peter.

5. THE GRANDEST GIFT OF JESUS

This is the most tender story in your book.

* * *

The Lord Jesus had washed the feet of the Apostles. Now they were all clean.

Jesus and the Apostles sat down again at the table.

Jesus was saying His last beautiful words to them. Before He died, He wanted to give them and us the grandest Gift in the world.

Suddenly Jesus took bread into His holy hands. Lifting up His eyes to heaven, Jesus blessed the bread. He broke It and gave It to His Apostles saying:

THIS IS MY BODY!

For the first time Jesus gave His Body to men as Food for their souls. It was the First Holy Communion of the Apostles.

Then Jesus took the chalice with wine. He blessed it and said:

THIS IS MY BLOOD!

He gave His Blood to the Apostles to drink.

JESUS AT THE LAST SUPPER

This was the First Holy Mass ever said on earth. Jesus told His Apostles to do what He had done—to change bread and wine into His Body and Blood. Jesus is Himself the Gift He promised. He will stay with men to the end of the world in the Holy Eucharist.

> I know who is hiding
> In the wee white Host.
> Jesus there is biding,
> He whom I love most.
>
> —*Father Faber*

SOMETHING TO DO

In your "I Believe Book" paste pictures of Holy Communion and of the Mass. Write three "I Believe" sentences.

or

Make a booklet of all the pictures you have on Holy Communion and on the Mass.

Write a little prayer to Jesus under each.

This will be your very own prayer book.

6. ON THE WAY TO THE MOUNT OF OLIVES

Read these stories which tell how much Jesus suffered for you. He did this because He loved you. Tell Jesus you will always love Him.

* * *

Jesus had said the first Mass. He had given us His great Gift. Now He was ready to open heaven, ready to die for us.

Jesus and His Apostles left the supper room. It was night. All was still, very still!

They walked to the Mount of Olives where Jesus loved to pray. On the way Peter said: "I will always be true to Jesus!"

But Jesus said sadly to Peter: "Peter, in this night thou wilt deny Me three times."

Peter said: "I will not deny Thee, Lord."

All the other Apostles spoke like Peter: "We will not deny Thee. We will never, never leave Thee."

7. ON THE MOUNT OF OLIVES

Jesus and the Apostles passed over a little brook and soon were on the Mount of Olives. Here, in a beautiful garden called Gethsemane, Jesus loved to pray.

Jesus said to the Apostles: "Stay here while I go farther on to pray."

Jesus prayed for three hours. He thought of all the sins of men. He thought of my sins, too. He prayed to His Father to forgive all men. He thought of His cruel death on the cross. Yes, soon Judas would come with soldiers to take Him and put Him to death. Even now, blood covered the whole body of Jesus because of His great fear.

It was near midnight.

The Apostles were all sleeping, but Jesus was still praying.

Oh! What was that noise? Why were those lights moving up the mountain side? Judas was coming! Judas, the wicked Apostle, was coming to catch the kind Master!

Jesus kept on praying. He knew what was going to happen. He was ready to die for all men.

At last Jesus rose from His prayer. Nearer

and nearer came Judas and the crowd of soldiers. Jesus watched them come up the mountain. The Apostles stood near Jesus.

Suddenly Judas, stepping out of the crowd, stood before Jesus.

"Hail!" he said to Jesus, and he kissed the holy face of the Lord. This kiss was the sign to the soldiers. Now they knew which one was Jesus.

"Friend," Jesus said kindly to Judas, "why hast thou come? Judas, dost thou betray the Son of Man with a kiss?"

The soldiers crowded about Jesus and bound Him with ropes. In terrible fear the Apostles ran away, leaving Jesus alone with His enemies.

Poor Jesus! All alone in the hands of the wicked soldiers! This was the will of His Father in heaven. It was also the will of Jesus, because He had come to die for all men.

SHOW ON THE SAND TABLE

The Mount of Olives, the Garden of Gethsemane, the brook, the path to Jerusalem.

8. JESUS BEFORE THE HIGH PRIEST

The soldiers led Jesus down the mountain side, over the brook, and along the road to Jerusalem. The enemies of Jesus were waiting in the city.

Soon Jesus, the Son of God, stood before the priests and the Pharisees, His enemies.

Jesus said nothing to them.

At last the High Priest cried out: "Art Thou Christ, the Son of the Living God?"

Jesus answered him in a loud voice: "I am!"

The High Priest tore his garments, saying: "Behold! now you have heard the blasphemy. What think you?"

But the priests and the Pharisees answered: "He is guilty of death."

In a moment the soldiers began to strike Jesus and to spit upon Him.

Jesus, gentle, loving Jesus, spoke not to them but suffered for our sins.

9. PETER DENIES CHRIST

But where were the Apostles of Jesus? Where was Peter? They said they would never leave Jesus. Poor Peter! He still loved His Jesus, but he was afraid of the Jews.

He followed far off in the crowd. He sat in the court of a High Priest, waiting to see what would happen to the Master.

Suddenly a maid servant said to Peter: "Art not thou one of His disciples?"

Peter, in great fear, denied it. He said, "I am not."

Soon another maid said to him: "Art not thou also one of His disciples?"

Peter again denied it, saying: "I am not."

It was cold and the soldiers had made a big fire in the yard. Peter stood at the fire warming himself. One of the soldiers said to him: "Surely thou art one of the disciples of Jesus."

In terrible fear Peter swore that he did not even know Jesus!

Peter for the third time denied his God!

Just at this moment Jesus was being led past the fire. The Lord Jesus, seeing Peter, looked at him. Peter then remembered what Jesus had said: "Peter, in this night thou shalt deny Me three times."

Peter went out, and began to weep bitterly.

All during that terrible night Jesus suffered and prayed for men.

10. JESUS BEFORE PILATE

It was early the next morning.

The enemies of Jesus led Him along the streets of Jerusalem. Many, many people followed them, but no one would help the suffering Jesus. They were afraid to help Him.

On, on, over to Pilate's palace the soldiers led Jesus. Pilate, the Roman Governor, alone could let them kill Jesus. That is why they took Jesus to Pilate.

Soon Jesus stood before Pilate, the Roman Governor.

Pilate was afraid of the people. He said to them: "What shall I do to the King of the Jews?" He meant Jesus.

"Crucify Him! Crucify Him!" the Jews answered in loud voices.

"What has He done that I should crucify Him?" he cried out to them.

They kept on shouting: "Crucify Him!"

Pilate gave Jesus to the cruel soldiers to be scourged by them. Blood covered the holy Body of Jesus after the wicked Jews had scourged Him.

JESUS BEFORE PILATE

That was not enough! The soldiers made a crown of thorns. They pushed it into the suffering head of Jesus.

  Jesus, by Thy holy Blood,
  Help, oh, help me to be good.

The soldiers then brought Jesus, covered with blood, back to Pilate. What a sad, sad scene. Pilate, filled with pity, showed the almost dead Jesus to the people.

"Behold the man," Pilate said to them.

"Crucify Him! Crucify Him!" shouted the cruel priests and people still louder.

Pilate gave Jesus to the Jews to be crucified by them. He washed his hands to show that he did not find any cause to crucify Jesus.

The Jews took Jesus out to Mount Calvary and they crucified Him, the Son of God!

SOMETHING TO WRITE

Write in your "I Believe Book" sentences using these words: Pilate, thorns, crucify, scourge, Judas, Blood, Calvary, Son of God.

11. JESUS ON THE CROSS

For three hours Jesus suffered on the cross. Read this little poem to your Jesus on the cross.

> Jesus, hanging on the cross,
>   Tell me, was it I?
> There are great big tear drops, Lord,
>   Did I make You cry?
>
> I have been a naughty child,
>   Naughty as can be;
> Now I am so sorry, Lord,
>   Won't You pardon me?

—*Father Tabb*

SOMETHING TO DO

Often kiss the feet of Jesus on your crucifix.

Kneel before Jesus on the cross every night.

Tell Him how sorry you are for all the sins of the day.

Tell father and mother to kneel before Jesus every night too.

Tell little sister and brother about Jesus on the cross.

12. JESUS, SAVIOR OF THE WORLD

For three long hours Jesus was hanging on the cross with nails in His hands and feet. He suffered all this to save the people of the world for heaven. For me, too, Jesus suffered, because He loved me.

During these long, long hours Jesus spoke such tender, holy words.

He prayed for His enemies, He prayed for me, too.

"Father," He said, "forgive them, for they know not what they do."

Two thieves were crucified with Jesus, one on the right and the other on the left of the Savior. The thief on the right was sorry for his sins. He asked Jesus to forgive them. Jesus said to him: "Today thou shalt be with Me in Paradise."

St. John, the beloved Apostle, stood at the cross of Jesus with the sad Mother Mary. Jesus looked lovingly upon them and said: "Mother, behold thy son. Son, behold thy

JESUS DIES ON THE CROSS

Mother." From that moment St. John took care of the Blessed Mother Mary.

Jesus suffered a terrible thirst. He cried out: "I thirst!" And the Jews gave Him vinegar to drink!

The life of Jesus was almost over. He had done the great work His Father wanted Him to do on earth. He spoke in a loud voice: "It is finished!"

Looking up to heaven once more, Jesus cried out in a loud voice: "Father, into Thy hands I commend My Spirit."

And bowing His head, the Lord Jesus, SAVIOR of the world, died upon the cross. This was the first Good Friday.

Suddenly the sun became dark. The earth shook. The dead rose from their graves and walked about. In fear all the Jews fled from Mount Calvary.

A soldier standing at the cross said: "This Man was the Son of God!"

Two good men took the Body of their Lord God down from the cross and put It into the arms of Mother Mary.

After a little while they placed the Body of Jesus in a tomb cut in a large rock.

13. IN LIMBO

Many good people had died since God had made the world. The gates of heaven were closed to them because Adam and Eve had sinned in Paradise. God made a place, called Limbo, where all these holy souls were waiting for the Savior. He would take them to heaven some day.

Suddenly, on the first Good Friday, the Soul of Jesus stood before them. Their Savior had come at last! He stayed with them for three days, telling them all about the wonderful story of His life and death.

How happy these holy souls in Limbo were! How happy Adam and Eve were, for now heaven was again open to all men.

> We adore Thee, O Christ,
> And we bless Thee,
> Because by Thy Holy Cross
> Thou has saved the world!

REVIEW TEST

Can you answer these questions?
Who is the Savior of the world?
Who is His Father?
Who is His mother?
Who is His foster father?
Was Jesus always God?
Was Jesus always man?
How long did Jesus live on earth?
Why did He live on earth so long?
Why did Jesus want to die for us?
Who betrayed Jesus?
What did Jesus suffer?
How did He die?
When did He die?
What were the words of Jesus on the cross?
How will you honor the crucifix?
What did Jesus give us at the Last Supper?
Is Jesus still with us?   Where?
How long will Jesus stay with us?

JESUS ARISES FROM THE DEAD

PART IX. THE MOST GLORIOUS STORY EVER TOLD

1. THE FIRST EASTER MORNING

This story tells you about the greatest miracle that ever happened. It shows to all men that Jesus is God!

* * *

It was very early morning the third day after Jesus' death.

The Body of the Lord was lying cold in the tomb. The Soul of Jesus came back to the tomb from Limbo. Suddenly the greatest miracle happened. The Soul of Jesus entered the dead Body, and Jesus Christ, the Savior of the World, rose from the dead!

He passed through the door of the tomb, and again the Lord Jesus walked upon the earth! This miracle is called the Resurrection of Jesus Christ. The Resurrection means that Christ raised Himself from the dead.

An angel of the Lord came down from heaven and rolled back the stone from the tomb. His face was like the lightning and his clothes were white as snow. For fear of Him the guards were struck with terror and became as dead men.

This was the first Easter Day. It was the day when Christ, true God and true Man, came back to life.

FILL IN THE SPACES

The Body of Jesus was lying dead in the ....

The Soul of Jesus was in........................

Christ rose from the dead on the................ day.

This great miracle is called the .... of Christ.

Christ is the .... of the world.

An....................rolled back the stone from the tomb.

The .... became as dead men.

Jesus Christ is true .... and true ....

2. JESUS AND HIS MOTHER

Whom do you think Jesus wished most to see? The story tells you about this visit.

* * *

The Mother of Jesus was praying early this first Easter morning.

Her heart was sad because her Jesus had been put to death so cruelly.

There was joy in her heart, too, for Jesus had saved the world! She knew that He would rise on the third day. He had told her so.

Suddenly a beautiful light filled her room. There stood the Lord Jesus!

"Mother!" He spoke sweetly to her, as she adored her glorious Son.

Only in heaven will we know the real joy of Mother Mary on this first Easter Day!

SOMETHING TO DO

Write a little letter to Jesus. Tell Him how much you love Him. Thank Him for saving the world, for saving you.

Write a little letter to Mother Mary, too.

Tell her how much you love her and Jesus. Ask her to take care of you always.

3. JESUS AND MARY MAGDALEN

Jesus appeared to the people He loved most. One of them was Mary Magdalen. Read the story and see how happy Jesus made her.

* * *

It was still early this first Easter morning.

The sun was shining gloriously in a beautiful blue sky, but Mary Magdalen was sad. She was weeping bitterly as she walked toward the tomb of Jesus. Oh, would He never, never again speak to her?

She reached the tomb. What had happened? The tomb was empty! The stone was rolled away! Jesus was gone!

Quickly Mary ran back to the Apostles in the city.

"They have taken the Lord away!" she cried out to them.

Peter and John hurried to the tomb with Mary. Yes, Jesus was gone! The two Apostles

rushed back to tell the others. Mary stood at the tomb, weeping.

Suddenly she saw two angels in white sitting in the tomb. They said to her: "Woman, why weepest thou?"

"Because they have taken away my Lord. I do not know where they have laid Him," she answered them.

The Gardener was passing by. Surely he would know what had happened to Jesus.

"Sir," she cried to him, "if thou hast taken Him away, tell me where thou hast laid Him. I will take Him away."

"Mary!" said the beautiful voice of Jesus. The Gardener was the Lord Jesus!

"Master!" Mary cried as she fell down at the feet of her Jesus and adored Him.

"Go tell My brethren: I ascend to My Father and to your Father, to My God, and to your God."

Mary ran with joy to give the grand message of Jesus to the Apostles.

SOMETHING TO DO

How many pictures can you see in this story? Talk about each one.

Build the tomb on the sand table. Make it very beautiful.

4. ON THE WAY TO EMMAUS

The Lord loved to surprise His friends. This story tells you how loving Jesus was to two of His disciples.

* * *

Evening of this first glorious Easter Day was near. Two of the disciples of Jesus were walking on the road from Jerusalem to a city called Emmaus. They were talking about the many things which had happened to Jesus. Their hearts were sad and lonely for their Master had been dead now three days.

As they were walking, Jesus Himself joined them on the way. The disciples did not know Him. They thought He was a stranger.

"What are you talking about, and why are you so sad?" Jesus asked them.

One of the men answered: "Art thou the only stranger in Jerusalem? Dost thou not know the things that have been done there in these days?" They told the Stranger about the life and death of their Lord.

When they came near the city, the sun was already setting.

The two disciples said to the Stranger: "Stay with us because it is toward evening." And He went in with them.

While they were at supper, the Lord Jesus took bread into His holy hands, just as He did at the Last Supper. He blessed It and gave It to them.

And suddenly the Stranger disappeared! Now the disciples knew the Stranger. He was the Lord Jesus! They knew Him in the breaking of the bread.

Quickly they ran back to Jerusalem and told the Apostles their wonderful story.

DO YOU KNOW:

When did Jesus say the First Mass?

What is Holy Communion?

When are bread and wine changed into the Body and Blood of Jesus?

Who says Holy Mass now?

Should a little child like you go to Mass often? Why do you think so?

5. THE NIGHT OF THE RESURRECTION

It was night of that first glorious Easter Day.

The Apostles, still in great fear of the Jews, were hiding from them. They had locked all the doors of their room. Only Thomas was not with them.

Suddenly Jesus stood before them. He had passed through the locked doors.

"Peace be to you!" were the kind words of the Lord.

The poor Apostles fell upon their knees. It was their own Jesus again!

"Peace be to you!" Jesus said again, and He breathed upon them. Then He said these holy words: "Receive ye the Holy Ghost. Whose sins you shall forgive, they are forgiven them! Whose sins you shall retain, they are retained!"

Then Jesus disappeared. Oh, how good the Savior was!

On the night before He died, Jesus gave us the Sacrament of the Holy Eucharist. On the night of His glorious Resurrection He gave us the Sacrament of Penance.

ANSWER THESE QUESTIONS

Who gave us the Sacraments?

What Sacrament did Jesus give us the night before He died?

What Sacrament did Jesus give us the night of His Resurrection?

When do we receive the Sacrament of the Holy Eucharist?

When do we receive the Sacrament of Penance?

Should a child receive the Sacrament of Penance often?

What does the Sacrament of Penance do for us?

What does the Sacrament of the Holy Eucharist do for us?

Must we be free from sin when we go to Holy Communion?

What must we do to receive Holy Communion worthily?

6. JESUS AND THOMAS

TIME: After the Resurrection of Jesus.

CHARACTERS: Jesus, Thomas, other Apostles.

Scene I. In a Locked Room

(*Thomas is with the other Apostles in the locked room. He does not believe that Jesus is living.*)

APOSTLE: Thomas, we have seen the Lord.

THOMAS: Except I shall see in His hands the print of the nails, and put my finger into the place of the nails, and put my hand into His side, I will not believe!

Scene II. The Same Locked Room

(*It is the next Sunday night. Thomas and the other Apostles are in the Upper Room. Suddenly Jesus stands before them.*)

JESUS: Peace be to you!

APOSTLES: It is the Lord! (*They kneel before Jesus.*)

JESUS (*to Thomas*): Put thy finger hither, and see My hands. Bring hither thy hand, and

put it into My side! and be not faithless but believing.

THOMAS (*filled with shame and fear*): My Lord and my God! (*Kneels before his God.*)

JESUS (*forgiving Thomas*): Thomas, because thou hast seen Me, thou hast believed. Blessed are they that have not seen, and have believed!

(*Thomas and all the Apostles are happy again with their Lord.*)

ANSWER YES OR NO

Did Jesus appear to the Apostles?

Was Thomas with them when Jesus appeared the first time?

Did Thomas believe the Apostles?

Was Thomas with the Apostles the next Sunday night?

Were the doors locked?

Did Jesus appear to them again?

Did Jesus open the doors to come in?

Did Jesus speak to Thomas?

Did Thomas now believe that Jesus was living?

Did Jesus forgive Thomas?

Was Thomas sorry for not believing the other Apostles?

Do you believe in Jesus?

7. JESUS IN GALILEE

It happened on the shore of a beautiful lake in Galilee.

One evening Peter said to the other Apostles: "I am going fishing!"

"We will go with you, Peter," they all said to him.

They sailed far out over the blue lake. The sun was just setting. It was a beautiful night.

The Apostles fished all the night, but they caught nothing.

Early the next morning they were near the shore across the lake, tired and hungry.

Somebody stood on the shore, watching them. "Children, have you anything to eat?" He asked them kindly.

They had to say no, because they had not caught any fish all that night.

"Cast your net on the right side of the ship!" the Man on the shore said to them.

They did so, and behold! at once their net was filled with many large, shining fish.

"It is the Lord!" John whispered to Peter. Peter at once jumped over the side of the boat and swam to Jesus.

Soon the ship had reached the shore and all the Apostles were with the Lord.

Jesus had made a bright fire on the shore. Here they fried the fish which they had caught, and had a very fine breakfast.

PICTURES

How many pictures do you see in this story? Talk about each one.

8. JESUS AND PETER

This story tells you how much Jesus loved Peter.

* * *

The fine breakfast on the seashore was over. Jesus stood up and called Peter to His side.

"Simon, Son of John, lovest thou Me?" Jesus asked Peter.

Peter answered the Lord with joy! "Lord, Thou knowest that I love Thee."

Jesus said to him: "Feed My Lambs!"
Again the Lord said to him: "Simon, Son of John, lovest thou Me?"

Peter wondered very much because Jesus had just asked him this question. He answered again: "Lord, Thou knowest that I love Thee."

Jesus said to him again: "Feed My Lambs!"

Jesus looked with love and pity on Peter and said a third time: "Simon, Son of John, lovest thou Me?"

Peter fell at the Lord's feet and answered: "Lord, Thou knowest all things. Thou knowest that I love Thee."

Jesus said to Peter: "Feed My Sheep!"

With these words Jesus made Peter the Head of His Church on earth. The sheep are the bishops of the Church, and the lambs are the people.

In that terrible night before Jesus died, Peter had denied the Lord three times. Now Peter told the whole world three times that he loved the Lord Jesus, his God, above all else.

How much Jesus loved Peter. He gave him all the sheep and all the lambs of the Catholic Church to care for.

SOMETHING TO DO

Write in your "I Believe Booklet" a sentence about each of these words: Resurrection, Easter, Savior, Miracle, Peter, Catholic Church, Bishop, Sheep, Lamb.

REVIEW TEST

Find the picture in your book or in the room which explains each sentence below. Tell the story in the picture.

Jesus Christ rose from the dead on Easter Morning.

The angel's face was like lightning and his clothes were white as snow.

Woman, why weepest thou?

Mary! Master!

My Lord and My God!

Feed My Lambs.

Whose sins you shall forgive, they are forgiven them.

Be not faithless but believing.

Stay with us.

JESUS ASCENDS INTO HEAVEN

PART X. THE HOLIEST STORY EVER TOLD

1. THE ASCENSION OF OUR LORD

Jesus stayed on earth forty days after His Resurrection to teach the Apostles about His Holy Church. Something wonderful happened on the last day He was on this earth. This story tells you.

* * *

It was a wonderful day. The sun was shining in a deep blue sky.

Jesus, Mary, the Apostles, and many other dear friends were on the beautiful Mount of Olives. Jesus was going home to heaven where His Father was waiting for Him. Today, too, all the souls from Limbo would enter heaven, to live in God's own home forever.

Jesus was speaking for the last time to His Apostles.

"Go ye into the whole world. Teach the Gospel to every creature," was His last command to the Apostles.

Jesus looked once more with love upon His holy Mother, upon His Apostles, upon all His friends. He looked over the whole world.

Suddenly Jesus began to raise Himself from the mountain. Up higher and higher into the blue sky He went. Stretching out His arms over the whole world, He blessed all, all! At last a white cloud hid the Lord Jesus from the eyes of men.

Behold! two angels in white stood by them. "You men of Galilee," they said to the friends of Jesus on the mountain, "why stand you here looking up to heaven? This Jesus shall so come again, as you have seen Him go into heaven."

This was the First Ascension Day, the day when Christ returned to His Father in heaven.

SOMETHING TO DO

With your book open at this lesson, ask your little friend questions about the Ascension of Jesus into heaven. Let your little friend ask you, too.

2. THE BIRTHDAY OF THE CHURCH

This story tells you about the Holy Ghost and about the Holy Roman Catholic Church.

* * *

Jesus had ascended into heaven.

Before He left His Apostles, He gave them another great Promise. He would send them the Holy Ghost from heaven. The Holy Ghost would teach them all they must know, and would keep them holy.

For nine days the Apostles waited and prayed for the Holy Ghost to come upon them. Mother Mary was with them in the Upper Room.

Suddenly there came a sound from heaven like a great wind. It filled the whole house.

The Holy Ghost came down upon the Apostles.

He came in the form of tongues of fire and rested upon each one of them.

People in the city heard the sounds and soon gathered in large crowds about the house.

Peter and the other Apostles were filled with the Holy Ghost. They opened the doors and began to preach the beautiful story of Jesus Christ.

By his holy words on this day, Peter taught three thousand people to believe in his Lord and Savior, Jesus Christ. These were the first Christians. This was the Grand Birthday of the Catholic Church.

The Holy Ghost will stay with the Church to the end of the world. He teaches through His Priests and Bishops and the Pope the Gospel of Jesus Christ. He leads the souls of men to their real home—Heaven!

ANSWER THESE QUESTIONS

Who is the Holy Ghost?
Who sent the Holy Ghost upon the Church?
Why did Jesus send the Holy Ghost?
How did the Holy Ghost come from heaven?

What did the Apostles do?
Who were the first Christians?
Are you a Christian?
What is the birthday of the Catholic Church?
How long will the Holy Ghost stay in the Church?
What does the Holy Ghost do in the Church?
What is your real home?

3. THE CATHOLIC CHURCH

The Catholic Church is the Kingdom of God.

The Catholic Church is in heaven, in purgatory, and on earth.

The saints belong to the Church in heaven. They pray for us on earth.

Good people, who have died with venial sins on their soul, belong to the Church in purgatory. Here they will suffer until their souls are pure in the eyes of God. Then God will take them to heaven. The souls in purgatory pray for us on earth.

All Catholic men, women, and children belong to the Church on earth. We pray to the angels and saints in heaven to ask God for His help. We pray for the poor souls in purgatory. We pray for all men on earth.

Jesus Christ is the Head of the Catholic Church in heaven, on earth, and in purgatory.

The Pope takes the place of Jesus Christ in the Church on earth.

The Catholic Church is the only true Church of God.

Put a line under the words that are correct in each sentence:

Now I belong to the Catholic Church (in purgatory, in heaven, on earth).

The saints belong to the Catholic Church (in purgatory, in heaven, on earth).

(We can help, we cannot help) the souls in purgatory.

Good people who die in venial sins, go (to heaven, to purgatory).

The souls in purgatory (suffer, do not suffer).

In heaven the saints (are happy, are not happy).

The souls in purgatory (pray for us, do not pray for us).

The Pope takes the place of Jesus Christ, (on earth, in heaven).

The Catholic Church is (the only, not the only) true Church of God.

4. MY CHURCH AND I

I belong to the kingdom of God on earth.

I am a prince in the kingdom of God.

I am happy and proud to be a Catholic child.

I will always be a Catholic.

I will die a Catholic with the help of God.

I will always love Mary, the Queen of the Catholic Church.

I will always serve Jesus Christ, the King of the Catholic Church.

....

(A Catholic Child)

5. MARY, QUEEN OF HEAVEN

This story tells you how the Blessed Virgin Mary went to God.

* * *

Some years had passed since Jesus had ascended into heaven. Mary, the Mother of Jesus, probably was now almost sixty-five years old. All these years she had been the Mother and Queen of the Apostles and of the first Christians.

How she loved them all, but she wished more and more to go to her Jesus in heaven.

One beautiful day Jesus called the soul of His Holy Mother to heaven.

Her holy body was placed in the tomb of the Apostles. Thomas was far away when his sweet Mother Mary died. How he wished once more to see her beautiful face, to kneel before her. Thomas came back to his dear friends, the other Apostles.

The Apostles were sorry for Thomas. Yes, they would open the tomb and let him see the body of his Mother Mary.

MARY, CROWNED QUEEN OF HEAVEN

They opened the tomb with great love and reverence.

Oh, the surprise! Oh, the joy! Instead of the dead body of their Mother, they saw pure lilies and beautiful roses! Jesus Christ had taken the body of His Mother to heaven, too. Before the angels and saints, He crowned His Mother with glory and made her the Queen of Heaven and Earth!

PRAYER

Hail, Holy Queen, Mother of Mercy,
Our life, our Sweetness, and our Hope!
To thee do we cry, poor banished children of Eve.
To thee do we send up our sighs,
Mourning and weeping in this valley of tears.
Turn, then, most gracious advocate, thine eyes of mercy toward us;
And after this our exile,
Show unto us the blessed Fruit of thy womb, Jesus,

O clement, O loving, O sweet Virgin Mary!
Pray for us, O holy Mother of God,
That we may be made worthy of the promises of Christ.

6. CHRIST, THE KING OF HEAVEN AND EARTH

O KING, LIVE FOREVER!

THOU ALONE ART MY KING AND MY GOD!

THIS IS GOD, OUR GOD UNTO ETERNITY, FOREVER.

HE SHALL RULE FOREVER AND EVER.

ALLELUJA!

CHRIST THE KING

WORD LIST

This word list contains the different words occurring in THE LIFE OF MY SAVIOR. The words which have been used in THE BOOK OF THE HOLY CHILD, Grade I, have been used freely and are not in this list. The words of the poems, the prayers, and the characteristically scriptural words, e.g., Jericho, High Priest, Hosanna, have not been included. Then also words which refer specifically to the Church, such as: purgatory, ascension, Eucharist, Communion, have also been omitted. They must naturally be found in their respective lessons and the teacher will help the pupil in a special manner to recognize these words. They do not, as a rule, occur in the Thorndike List of Words.

The words in the list are arranged by pages and are marked according to the system used in E. L. Thorndike's THE TEACHER'S WORD BOOK. Those from the first 500 words in most common use in reading matter are marked 1a; those from the second 500 are marked 1b; those from the third 500 are marked 2a; those from the fourth 500 are marked 2b, and so forth.

Numbers not followed by letters are credit-numbers, and indicate the importance of the words. Words having a credit-number of 9 are found between the 5145th and the 5544th word in importance; those with 8, between the 5545th and the 6047th; with 6, between the 6619th and the 7262nd; with 5, between the 7263rd to 8145th; with 4, between the 8146th and the 9190th; and with 3, beween 9191 and 10,000.

11				17		25		34	
earth	1a	seven	1b	fifteen	2a	forty	2a
read	1a	eyes	1a	happen	1b	moment	1b
alone	1a	hands	1a	quiet	1b	36	
suddenly	1b	serve	1a	26		character	2a
forever	3b			bow	1b	desert	2a
12		19		believe	1a	camel	4b
sister	1a	poem	3a	27		37	
brother	1a	close	1a	lady	1b	wicked	2b
13		beside	1b	country	1a	38	
world	1a	angel-folk	2a	ready	1a	city	1a
14		instead	1b	29		palace	2a
dark	1a	20		hurry	1b	raising	1a
light	1a	promise	1b	command	1b	39	
hill	1a	devil	2b	clothes	1b	dream	1b
write	1a	die	1a	30		draw	1a
body	1a	22		inn	3b	41	
15		hide	1a	31		cruel	2a
ribs	3a	closed	1a	arms	1a	quickly	1a
breathe	2a	gates	1b	wrapped	2b	43	
sand	1b	23		33		live	1a
16		thousand	1a	twinkling	3b	44	
whole	1a			appear	1b	sorrow	2a
				lying	2a		

193

47		**62**		**76**		**94**	
sitting	1a	waiters	7	street	1a	dash	2a
48		pots	2a	whispered	2a	torn	3a
remember	1a	carry	1b	laugh	1a	ghost	2b
thirty	2a	chief	1b	**77**		shouted	1b
49		steward	6	space	1b	wild	1b
suffer	1b	**63**		**78**		**96**	
cross	1a	tasted	1b	weep	2a	jump	1b
50		changed	1a	**81**		wave	1b
held	1b	**64**		mile	1a	**97**	
question	1b	servant	2a	**82**		match	2a
game	1b	sick	1b	change	1a	**98**	
53		officer	1b	necessary	1b	fold	2a
public	1b	army	1b	**83**		**99**	
behold	2b	**66**		message	2a	richest	1a
55		answer	1a	enemies	1b	pastures	2b
open	1a	worthy	2a	**85**		wolves	2a
form	1a	heal	3a	brave	1b	bush	2a
dove	3a	**67**		**86**		**101**	
sentence	3a	cripple	4b	tomb	3b	counting	1a
paste	5b	proud	1b	bound	2a	forgave	5
56		yard	1b	white	1a	**102**	
hungry	2a	roof	1b	cloth	1b	neighbor	1b
stones	1a	plan	1b	forth	1b	lawyer	2b
bread	1a	**69**		loose	2a	write	1a
better	1a	rope	2b	**87**		**103**	
57		surprise	1b	review	2b	band	1b
tempt	3a	forgiven	3a	test	2b	robber	3a
proud	1b	**70**		**89**		hide	1b
mountain	1a	blind	1b	trip	1b	wounded	2a
58		mercy	2b	sailed	1a	**104**	
apostles	4	**71**		**90**		horse	1a
chosen	2a	voice	1a	hundred	1a	money	1a
catch	1b	**72**		broke	2b	need	1a
fish	1b	lepers	5	sank	4a	**105**	
boat	1b	cave	2b	depart	2a	silks	1b
59		covered	1a	sinful	9	**106**	
left	1a	sores	2b	ending	5a	points	1a
60		lame	3a	**91**		leaves	1a
net	2a	**73**		storm	1b	**107**	
call	1a	priest	3a	terrible	2a	pieces	1a
four	1a	face	1a	black	1a	hell	3b
shore	1b	eighth	3a	**93**		**108**	
61		ninth	3a	wind	1a	bosom	2b
miracle	4a	tenth	3a	blew	3a	drink	1a
wedding	4b	**75**		master	1b	finger	1b
music	1b	daughter	1b	manner	1b	tongue	1b
wine	2a						
hour	1a						

109		**128**		**151**		**168**	
elder	3b	merciful	9	enough	1a	lock	2a
prodigal	6	**131**		thorns	2b	receive	1a
stranger	2b	donkey	4a	push	2a	retain	3b
porch	2b	palm	3a	heard	1a	**170**	
110		**132**		cause	1a	except	1b
pigs	2a	welcome	2a	**154**		print	2a
kisses	1a	hated	2a	hanging	1b	hither	3a
112		**133**		nails	2a	**171**	
shoes	1b	already	1b	beloved	3b	faithless	8
feet	1a	den	3a	**155**		shame	2a
calf	4a	thief	3a	thirst	2b	**173**	
114		**135**		vinegar	5a	cast	2a
grade	2b	willing	2b	almost	1a	**174**	
station	1b	mortal	2b	finish	1b	swam	9
program	5b	**137**		commend	3b	fry	5a
speaker	3b	washes	1b	spirit	1b	**176**	
115		dish	2a	Friday	2a	bishop	4b
Tuesday	2b	move	1a	shook	2b	**180**	
o'clock	3a	**142**		graves	1b	creature	2a
117		deny	2b	**160**		stretch	2a
kingdom	2a	**143**		lightning	3a	cloud	1b
118		brook	1b	guard	1b	**181**	
line	1a	farther	2a	struck	2b	lesson	1b
naughty	4b	death	1a	terror	2b	sound	1a
120		noise	1b	**161**		**182**	
commandment	9	**145**		wish	1a	rested	1a
perfect	1b	sign	1b	letter	1a	preach	2b
121		betray	3a	**162**		birthday	2b
loaves	4b	path	1b	empty	2a	**183**	
grass	1b	**146**		**163**		pure	1b
122		loud	1b	rush	1b	**184**	
gather	1b	strike	1b	**164**		correct	2a
baskets	1b	spit	4b	gardener	1a	**185**	
flesh	2a	**148**		brethren	4a	pope	3b
123		fire	1a	ascend	3a	**186**	
unless	2a	swore	5b	**165**		prince	1b
tiptoes	3	**149**		lonely	4a	queen	1b
125		bitter	2a	join	1b	**187**	
hardly	2a	crucify	4	**166**		sixty-five	3a
golden	1b	scourge	4b	setting	1a	**189**	
				167		reverence	4a
				disappeared	2b	lily	3a
						rose	1b

www.ingramcontent.com/pod-product-compliance
Lightning Source LLC
Chambersburg PA
CBHW042132160426
43199CB00021B/2886